EXTRAORDINARY
LEADERSHIP

JOSEPH K. PHETO

authorHOUSE

AuthorHouse™ UK
1663 Liberty Drive
Bloomington, IN 47403 USA
www.authorhouse.co.uk
Phone: 0800 047 8203 (Domestic TFN)
+44 1908 723714 (International)

© 2019 Joseph K. Pheto. All rights reserved.

No part of this book may be reproduced, stored in a retrieval system, or transmitted by any means without the written permission of the author.

Published by AuthorHouse 10/18/2019

ISBN: 978-1-5462-9830-4 (sc)
ISBN: 978-1-5462-9829-8 (e)

Print information available on the last page.

Any people depicted in stock imagery provided by Getty Images are models, and such images are being used for illustrative purposes only.
Certain stock imagery © Getty Images.

This book is printed on acid-free paper.

Because of the dynamic nature of the Internet, any web addresses or links contained in this book may have changed since publication and may no longer be valid. The views expressed in this work are solely those of the author and do not necessarily reflect the views of the publisher, and the publisher hereby disclaims any responsibility for them.

CONTENTS

Chapter 1   Introduction 1

Chapter 2   Foundations of Great Leadership 5

Chapter 3   Misconceptions about Leadership 16

Chapter 4   Personal Leadership 23

Chapter 5   Good Employment Is Key 32

Chapter 6   Create and Instil a Great Vision 40

Chapter 7   Good Governance and Accountability 45

Chapter 8   Relationship Management 57

Chapter 9   Exercise Good Human Resources Principles ... 68

Chapter 10 Develop Good Interpersonal Skills 93

Chapter 11 Drive for Results 112

Chapter 12 Effective Performance Management 121

Chapter 13 Effective Delegation 130

Chapter 14 Giving Effective Feedback 136

Chapter 15 Talent Management and Succession Planning............ 147

Chapter 16 Effectively Leading Teams 165

Chapter 17 Fostering Innovation... 169

Chapter 18 Leave a Great Legacy 184

References 191

About the Author 193

CHAPTER 1
INTRODUCTION

Leadership is a word that is often misused in operational and training circles. A lot of people misconstrue the word to mean worshipping those who have been placed in leadership positions. The reverse of this is when those in leadership positions expect to be worshipped because they are at the helm. This principle held true when the workforce was made up of employees who had lower levels of education, knowledge, and general awareness. There was also a religious component to consider when assessing leaders such as Jesus Christ and Moses.

Another misconception regarding the word *leadership* is that the majority of people believe that only a small portion of the population are born with leadership abilities. "Leaders are born" is a common expression. During my leadership training workshops, I am frequently asked, "Are leaders born or developed?" What is quite intriguing is that no one ever asks, "Are managers born or developed?" Why is it that management is viewed as a trainable skill set, while leadership is typically seen as an innate personality trait? It's simple: People assume that management can be taught, and they are correct. Hundreds of business schools have been established, and each year they teach thousands of management courses. By assuming that people can develop the attitude and skills necessary to be a successful manager, schools and companies have improved the overall quality of management. They have contributed to the idea that good management skills are attainable. The same is true about leadership. It has been proven that everyone has the potential to become an effective leader. The only difference is in whether or not an individual receives an opportunity to demonstrate his or her leadership qualities.

Rather than viewing leadership as an innate character trait—which has become a self-fulfilling prophecy that dooms society to having only a few good leaders—it is far safer, healthier, and more productive to assume that it's possible for anyone to learn how to be a leader. By assuming that leadership is teachable, we can discover how many good leaders go unrecognised. Somewhere, sometime, the leader within each of us may get the call to step forward—for our schools, for our congregations, for our communities, for our agencies, for our companies, for our unions, for our political parties, or for our countries. It is our responsibility to be prepared to receive that call. Ordinary people can become extraordinary leaders. Those who are most successful at bringing out the best in others are those who set achievable stretch goals. Effective leaders are constantly learning; they are constantly looking for ways to improve themselves and their organisations. By engaging in personal development activities, one demonstrates a disposition to lead. In order to become a good leader, one must believe in his or her abilities.

There is another myth that stands in the way of personal and organisational success. It's the myth that leadership is associated with a person's professional title. It is assumed that leadership starts with a capital *L* and that being on top automatically makes someone a leader. It's part of a larger hero myth that inhibits us from seizing the initiative. "It's not my job," we say, waiting for someone to ride in and save us. Well, forget it. This premise is just a myth. Leadership is not limited to one person or one position. It is also not limited to genetics or to some secret code that is only available to a few individuals. The real truth is that leadership can be developed. It is a set of skills and abilities that can be taught and coached. Anybody can learn how to become a leader. In the same vein, leadership is a skill that can be strengthened, honed, and enhanced. One just needs the desire and the motivation to do so. One needs to practise the best principles and accept feedback to continually build one's skill sets. One can also emulate a role model's behaviour or look to a mentor for guidance.

Some people misinterpret leadership as a popularity contest, where the most popular individuals are expected to take up leadership roles. We see this misconception a lot in politics. It is easy to mistake charisma for leadership.

To avoid getting caught in this conundrum, we use adjectives like *effective*, *outstanding*, and *extraordinary* to describe the leadership qualities organisations and institutions look for in potential applicants. This is the kind of leadership that inspires subordinates to deliver positive results.

What Is Leadership?

Leadership is the ability to influence others in order to achieve organisational goals. In his book, The Leader Who Had No Title, author Robin Sharma once said, "Growing and developing leadership talent of every single person throughout the organisation faster than the competition is the only way to avoid getting eaten alive." Leadership experts and researchers around the world have agreed that investing in leadership development is crucial to the success of any business. This becomes an ongoing process, as leadership development takes time and patience.

In today's workplace, leaders at all levels face enormous challenges to achieve and sustain breakthrough results. Globalisation, economic change, stringent regulations, and government interference make realising shareholder value increasingly difficult.

Leadership is defined as top executives who have displayed high levels of persistence, overcome significant obstacles, attracted dedicated people, influenced groups of people towards the achievement of a common goal, and played key roles in guiding their companies through crucial moments.

John Mattone asserts that outstanding leadership has a strong inner core—that is, character, values, positive beliefs, positive emotions, and self-concept. This inner core will be demonstrated by

- a powerful sense of vision;
- strong belief and faith in that vision;
- optimism and enthusiasm;
- a strong ability to handle complexity, uncertainty, and ambiguity;
- a strong ability to view temporary failures as opportunities for greater effort or innovation;
- character traits of honesty, modesty, humility, diligence, focus, and courage;
- the ability to empower others;
- an individual's passion, drive, and incredible zeal; and
- a strong sense of accountability.

CHAPTER 2

FOUNDATIONS OF GREAT LEADERSHIP

The foundation of great leadership is derived from leadership that aims to establish sustained superior performance over a long period of time. This kind of performance must be nurtured by a winning culture of unleashed people. It is achieved by great leaders who know how to unlock the potential in the majority of their constituents. This is the kind of culture where people are excited to serve the organisation and deliver high-quality products and services. This kind of performance and culture results in customers who not only are loyal but also are partners and promoters of the organisation.

Great leadership starts by being aware and being able to differentiate between leadership, management, and supervision. This differentiation ensures a streamlined approach to a company's management structure. I meet a lot of people who think leadership and management are one and the same. Leadership is different from management, but not for the reasons most people think. From a modern human perspective, good leadership has nothing to do with popularity, charisma, or fear. It is an attainable skill that anyone can acquire through ambition and discipline. Leadership is not reserved for the chosen few. It is not in any way better than management. It does not replace management. Both traits coexist and complement each other. Institutions require competent leadership, competent management, and competent supervision. If a manager displays incompetence in any of these areas, there will be chaos in the institution. Leadership is the ability to influence others in order to achieve organisational or institutional goals. Good leaders do this by motivating and inspiring their constituents. The use of fear and coercion is not in their formula. On the other hand, management is the ability to control and maintain plans, budgets, resources, processes, systems, and procedures. Managers are in a leadership position. Supervision is the ability to control the workplace. Supervisors play a lesser leadership role.

Most corporations are overmanaged and underled. This means that they have too much management and very little leadership. Corporations facing this challenge need to develop the capacity to exercise leadership. Successful corporations don't wait for leaders to come along. They take proactive measures to develop leadership at various levels of the organisation. They actively seek out people with leadership potential and expose them to career experiences designed to develop that potential. With careful selection, nurturing, and encouragement, dozens of people can play important leadership roles in any situation.

Companies should remember that strong leadership with weak management is no better—it is actually worse than the reverse. The real challenge is in combining strong leadership with strong management. It is crucial to maintain this balance. Of course, not everyone can be a good manager *and* a good leader. Some people have the capacity to be excellent managers but not strong leaders. Smart companies value both kinds of employees, and they work hard to build a balanced team.

When it comes to preparing people for executive roles, recent studies suggest that people who cannot manage and lead should be ignored. Once companies understand the fundamental difference between management and leadership, they can begin to groom their top people to display both qualities.

Extraordinary leaders need to have grit. They need to be inordinately persistent and wildly courageous. They need to take far more risks than any ordinary person. That is not as hard as it might sound. Everyone has a well of courage just begging to be tapped. We all want to be superheroes in some form or another, and we have the capacity of character to keep going when everyone around us is ready to give up.

Toughness, guts, and courage come from consistent development and positive experience. It does not naturally come to an individual, but it is built over time. Well-developed leaders see opportunities others don't see. Where others see challenges, they see opportunities. They are also able to see around corners. These kinds of leaders create great visions, and they passionately fall in love with their visions. Nobody can divert them from their goal. They believe in the secret inner power that all great leaders share. Their wisdom gives them guts, which in turn develops into courage. When incompetent leaders are at the helm, employees will notice their resolve weaken when the going gets tough. They make everyone panic or lose trust in their leadership. That is why I advise organisations to hire or promote leaders who display a good balance of intellect and leadership.

A lot of people who were led by great leaders always claim that those leaders engaged them. They say that their leaders respected them. This also indicates that these leaders trusted their subordinates, so their subordinates trusted them as well. The great leaders are also said to care about and pay attention to their subordinates. These are the kinds of leaders who believe in their subordinates. They make their subordinates feel like they contribute to the results of the organisation. These kinds of leaders also value diversity. They make their employees feel like they are important. They solicit ideas, and they empower everybody. These kinds of leaders put the company first and practise professional will. They practise humility and have an unwavering resolve to deliver results for the organisation. They give credit for good results. They focus on both long-term and short-term goals. These kinds of leaders also place a lot of value on self-development.

Joseph K. Pheto

Moral Authority Is Key

Wisdom is the effective and beneficial use of information, knowledge, talents, skills, and experience for the achievement of a greater good. Wisdom is living life with principles and with a higher purpose to serve humanity. It is about respecting or seeing value or potential in each individual. Wisdom is also about celebrating diversity and the differences in people. It is in the knowing that each different opinion has a chance of adding value to the institution. Wisdom is about the discipline to serve the institution as opposed to serving oneself. Wisdom is always guided by one's moral compass. This then brings with it the value of moral authority, which is largely based on ethics and accountability. Leaders with moral authority are highly respectable and leave a lasting positive legacy. If you do not agree with me, just start comparing a Nelson Mandela with an Adolf Hitler. You will notice the difference.

Moral authority might sound like a contradiction in terms. The word *authority* may make one think of things like command, control, power, sway, rule, supremacy, domination, dominion, strength, and might. The word *moral* adds all sorts of things like righteousness, nobility, justice, fairness, and truthfulness. But the antonym is civility, servitude, weakness, and followership. Moral authority can therefore be explained as the kind of leadership that endeavours to follow principles. It views the role of leadership as one of servanthood, service, and contribution. The power of moral authority comes from the notion of the leader subordinating himself or herself to the people as opposed to being served. Servant leaders command respect even from those people who oppose them. When you think of people like Nelson Mandela, you will notice this kind of moral authority we are talking about where the leader regards himself as a servant of the people.

In his book Good to Great, author Jim Collins puts it this way: "The most powerfully transformative executives possess a paradoxical mixture of personal humility and professional will. They are timid and ferocious.

Shy and fearless. They are rare—and unstoppable ... good to great transformations don't happen without level five leaders at the helm, they just don't." These kinds of leaders know how to create a balance between moral authority and formal authority.

Leadership success lies at the intersection of excellence and honour. Nowadays, people in business like to cut corners. And they think only of themselves. But one thing to know is that even one breach of our ethics will pollute everything we touch. Nothing is more precious in work than staying consistent with your values and protecting your good name. In so many ways, your reputation is all you have.

Shortcomings of Leadership

After going through a staggering amount of research (in Stephen R. Covey's *The 8th Habit*) that was done by Harris Interactive, I wondered, *Just what has gone wrong?* Following are the results of this research:

- Only 37 per cent of the workforce understands what their organisation exists for or envisions to achieve.
- Only 20 per cent of the workforce are committed to and enthusiastic about achieving their team's and organisation's goals.
- Only 20 per cent of the workforce have absolute clarity about their team's and organisation's goals and how their daily tasks contribute to those goals.
- Only 50 per cent of the workforce have satisfaction in their work and their normal weekly accomplishments.
- Only 15 per cent of the workforce feel that their organisation allows them to use their intelligence to execute key organisational goals.
- Only 15 per cent of the workforce feel there is a high level of trust in their organisation.

- Only 17 per cent of the workforce feel their organisation practises open communication and collaboration and that diversity and differences in opinion are valued.
- Only 10 per cent of the workforce feel that their organisation equally holds all individual employees accountable for results.
- Only 20 per cent of the workforce fully trust the organisation they work for.
- Only 13 per cent of the workforce feel that their organisation exhibits silo thinking and that there are no high-trust or conducive relationships with other groups or departments in their organisation.

If these scores represented soccer playing, a competitive game, only four of the eleven players on the field would know where they were scoring. Only two of the eleven would really want to win. Only two of the eleven would know the position they were to play and what their contribution would be. And nine of the eleven players would be competing against the remaining two players rather than against the opponent. This is absolutely shocking to take in.

Arnold Toynbee was quoted as saying, "Nothing fails like success." This translates to the fact that when you have a challenge and you come up with a response that is equal to the challenge, this is viewed as success. But once you have a new challenge, the old and previously successful response will no longer work. It will now be viewed as a failure. For some reason, most leaders have adopted the type of leadership style that was successful in the industrial age. In the industrial age, the mode of leadership was controlling in nature—the only way to get work done was to control the workers. The workers were never expected to give advice or opinions on the way the work could best be done. Now we live in a knowledge worker age, but the irony is that most leaders still use the tactics of industrial age leadership where they continue to control the workers to get the work done. Unfortunately for this sort of leader, today's workers are knowledgeable and want to be engaged and given the opportunity to use their intelligence to innovate and get things done their own way. In simple terms, what used to be successful in the industrial age can no longer be successful in the knowledge worker age. A new mindset is required for success in this new era. You as a leader need to adopt principles that unleash human potential.

Sometimes people ask me questions like, "What do you do with people who need to be controlled?" Nobody needs to be controlled. Just inspire them to see the worth in themselves. There will be those with a bad attitude, of course, who might need to be corrected or otherwise shown the door. If that is what is being called for, then do it timeously. Just know that when you manage people like things, they stop believing that leadership is really a choice that people can make to learn the skills required to lead well.

Leadership really has nothing to do with a position, so I encourage everyone to see themselves as a leader regardless of whether they have a leadership position or not. Everyone must know that decisions about what must be done in an organisation are not only the preserve of those in positions of authority. Just know that every individual has the potential to contribute immensely to the success of the organisation, and hence they do not deserve to be treated like things. You will only be doing yourself a favour by seeing yourself as a value adder in everything that your organisation is doing. Do not hesitate; take the initiative and act. Never wait to be told what to do by a person with a formal title. Behave as a CEO wherever you are in the organisational structure. Be accountable for results even when things go wrong. Give yourself credit when things go well. Thank yourself for cooperating and supporting the rest of the team.

Great leaders need to change the culture of control into a culture of personal management and individual contribution. In the latter type of culture, people must take the initiative and act independently without being managed or controlled. Subordinates do not have to be controlled to deliver results. Those who need to be controlled are very bad employees in this knowledge worker era. Managers who want to control really do not have a place in this era. A manager should hire smart people and allow them to perform in their own way. Your job as a manager is to inspire and release more potential in your subordinates. In the modern era, we no longer need a codependent culture where managers want to control and where subordinates expect to be controlled. People must unconsciously expect to perform independently.

Most of the leaders I have worked with my entire life were the controlling type of leaders. I started my career in the mining industry, which at the time was transitioning from an industrial type of operation to a knowledge type of operation. It was an era where most of the leadership positions were filled with university graduates as opposed to traditional long-term service-experienced personnel who were very used to the controlling culture. That was also the time when technology was rapidly becoming a means to production. During the same period I was engaged with an NGO that was teaching and developing leadership to young people. This then created a serious misalignment between what I was observing at work and what I was learning from my leadership development organisation. My learnings were also verified by the new books on leadership that were entering the market. From that point on, I became an advocate of knowledge worker age leadership.

My contention is that knowledge workers need to be unleashed and empowered as opposed to being controlled. You inform them of the results you are after, and then you allow them to figure out how to produce those results. You then evaluate their performance through the 360-degree appraisal system. It is wrong and insulting to control and micromanage knowledge workers. But in case you find yourself having to do such a thing, there are two possibilities—either you lack knowledge of the new leadership mindset and skill set, or you have bad-quality employees who are mismatched to the job. If you have hired knowledge workers with the right attitude, you do not have to manage them but may allow them to manage themselves. The only thing you can manage is their performance in producing results.

I agree with Stephen Covey that we can compare this controlling style of leadership with the bloodletting of the Middle Ages. The problem I have noticed in most organisations I have worked with is that they hire incompetent leaders and then teach them or reward them for leading by using the controlling mindset to the point that it is the only thing they know. We can compare this with what doctors used to practise to try to heal diseases in olden times. They were taught to use bloodletting to heal every disease. The idea was that germs had gotten into the blood and hence needed to be removed. That was the only thing they knew. Some of today's leaders treat people as things and then control them.

Now let's take a look at how things will be done in the new knowledge worker age—an employee will be respected as a whole person doing a whole job. Employees will be paid fairly, treated kindly, used creatively, and given opportunities to serve human needs in principled ways. This is what must happen with modern leaders, a total change in paradigm. They must be taught that that need hire to good-quality knowledge workers who must be unleashed and empowered as opposed to being controlled. Then the leader must try to follow all the effective leadership skills described in the rest of *Extraordinary Leadership*. In Richard and Daniel Goleman's book *Resonant Leadership*, they research have indicated the following:

- Fifty per cent of leaders in most organisations detract from the value of their organisations.
- Seventy per cent of leaders are not adding value to the organisation (they want to fit in and want to be a good corporate citizen, so they emulate the people around them).
- Fifty-three per cent of Fortune 500 CEOs do not have the skills they need to lead their organisations.

This resonates quite well with what we notice in the rest of the world.

This silent conspiracy is everywhere. Not many people are brave enough to even recognise it in themselves. Whenever they hear the idea, they instinctively look outside themselves.

Table 2.1 **Characteristics of great leaders and bad leaders**

Great leaders	Bad leaders
Engage me	Do not listen
Respect me	Are racist/tribalistic/discriminatory
Trust me, so I trust them	Are disempowering
Pay attention to me	Hire and fire
Care about me	Bully
Cause me to believe in them	Do not care for me
Make me feel like I contribute	Lack fairness
Value diversity	Are irresponsible
Make me feel like what I do is important	Are unaccountable
	Are incompetent
Are good with feedback	Lack confidentiality
Solicit ideas	Lack support
Empower me	Pass the buck
Put the company first	Are negative
Practise professional will	Are demeaning
Practise humility	Are deceitful
Have unwavering resolve	Are self-centred
Give credit for good results	Do not put the company first
Take the blame for bad results	Are narrow-minded
Are focused on the long term vs the short term	Are only interested in numbers and tasks and not me
Value self-development	Practise favouritism
	Lie
	Cheat
	Are boring
	Do not enjoy what they do
	Micromanage
	Focus on the details of my work
	Do not allow me to do what I am supposed to do
	Are always finding fault

Bad Leaders

They do not listen. They are discriminatory, tribalistic, or racist. They disempower. They characterise themselves as people who hire and fire. They are bullies. They do not care for their subordinates. They lack fairness and justice. They are irresponsible and unaccountable. They are incompetent. They lack support and confidentiality. They pass the buck. They are negative in everything. They are narrow-minded. They are demeaning and deceitful. They are self-centred and do not put the company or organisation first. They are only interested in tasks and numbers and are not interested in employees. They practise favouritism. They lie and cheat. They do not enjoy what they are doing and are boring people. They micromanage their juniors. They are always focused on details of the work and are always finding fault. They do not allow their subordinates to do what they are supposed to do. I bet this sounds familiar as there is bad leadership in most organisations.

Great Leaders

You can contrast the above with what great leaders do. They engage their employees. They respect and trust their employees. They care about them and give them attention when they need it. They believe in their employees and support them. They treat them as contributors and make them feel as if their work is important to the institution. They solicit ideas from subordinates and give constructive feedback. They value diversity, and they empower all their subordinates. They always put the interests of the institution ahead of their own interests. They are principled and humble. They have the professional will to do their work and have an unwavering resolve to deliver results. They give credit for good results and take the blame for bad results. They value self-development and the development of their team. They focus both on the long term and the short term.

CHAPTER 3

MISCONCEPTIONS ABOUT LEADERSHIP

A lot of leaders associate leadership with the position they hold. Leadership is more about who you are and the kind of actions you take than the position you hold. Who you are as a person comes from the development and grooming you go through to become a leader. The kind of actions you take comes from knowing what makes people tick. The old paradigm of command and control is obsolete at high levels of leadership in the modern era. There are a lot of problems caused by leaders who use control as a tool for leading their organisation.

Table 3.1 **Industrial age leadership versus knowledge worker age leadership**

Issue	Old industrial age control model	New knowledge worker age release/empowerment model
Leadership	A position (formal authority)	A choice (moral authority)
Management	Control things and people	Control things, release (empower) people
Structure	Hierarchical, bureaucratic	Flat, boundary-less, flexible
Motivation	External, carrot-and-sticking	Internal—whole person

Performance appraisal	External, sandwich technique	Self-evaluation using 360° feedback
Information	Primarily short-term financial reports	Balanced scorecard (long and short term)
Communication	Primarily top-down	Open: up, down, sideways
Culture	Social rules/mores of the workplace	Principle-centred values and economic rules of the marketplace
Budgeting	Primarily top-down	Open, flexible, synergistic
Training and development	Sideshow, skill-oriented, expendable	Maintenance, strategic, whole person, values
People	Expense on P & L, asset lip service	An investment with the highest leverage
Voice	Generally unimportant for most	Strategic for all, complementary to the team

Source: Stephen R. Covey, *The 8th Habit* (New York: Free Press, 2004), 245.

Old Industrial Age Control Model Leadership

Old-school leaders think leadership is associated with the position. They want to control things, and they also want to control people. They prefer hierarchical, bureaucratic structures. Their employee motivation style is carrot-sticking. The performance appraisal they use is external, the sandwich technique. Communication and budgeting are primarily top-down, and lower employees are not expected to contribute ideas. These types of leaders are only focused on short-term financial goals. They create a dysfunctional culture of social rules and mores in the workplace. People, and training and development of employees, are seen as an expense and are given asset lip service.

The carrot-and-stick method of motivation combines rewards and punishment to guide behaviour in the workplace. It is the mentality of certain managers and leaders to think they will use the carrot and stick to shape employee behaviour. This style of employee motivation has its source in the leader's incompetence. These managers try to entice their juniors with rewards like employment favours and with punishments like demotion. The term historically comes from when a cart driver would, from behind, dangle a carrot from a stick in front of the mule. The mule was expected to move towards the carrot because it wanted to be rewarded with food, and at the same time it wanted to move away from the stick behind the carrot it since it did not want such a punishment. In the process, the mule will pull the cart as the driver required.

This method is in complete contrast to engaging people with potential and creating an environment that releases their potential to allow for inner self-fulfilment once performance has been achieved. The carrot-and-stick mentality is so toxic in organisations as it is normally practised by incompetent managers and leaders solely for their own selfish needs, as opposed to being practised to meet organisational needs. A lot of managers and leaders use this method to address their own insecurities and fears of the employees they perceive to be smarter than them. Sometimes the carrot will be placed very far out of reach until the incompetent manager feels he or she has achieved the behaviour sought.

New Knowledge Worker Age Leadership Model

Leadership is principle-centred and viewed as service. Leaders control things, but they do not control people—instead they release and empower people. They prefer a flat, boundary-less structure. They allow their employees to be motivated internally through self-fulfilment. They use or apply self-evaluation appraisal using the 360-degree feedback system. The results and information is communicated using the balanced scorecard system covering long-term and short-term goals. Communication is open—it can be up, down, or sideways. Leaders encourage an effective culture that is inspired by principle-centred values and the economic rules of the marketplace. Budgeting is open, flexible, and synergistic. People, and training and development, are seen as an investment with the highest leverage.

Problems with the Controlling Style of Leadership

The problem with the control style of leadership is that such leaders tend to treat their leadership as being associated with the position. For them, it becomes easy to define leadership by their position. One of the ills I have seen in my own country, which I am sure is the case in many other countries, is the arbitrary promotion of people to leadership positions who have no leadership ability. If you do not have good leadership knowledge and experience, you can very easily adopt this obsolete control model of leadership when facing the challenges that you and your organisation will experience. The first thing is that you will rely on your position as your security, and the rest of your leadership decisions will be defined by the position. You will think that once you have the position or title, people will always identify with you. However, this is a myth.

As indicated above, the problem with these immature leaders is that they define leadership by their position. Their thinking is that once they have a position or title, people will identify with them. However, positions and titles can be misleading. A position always promises more than it can deliver. In being given a position, leadership is given to you, but your most important job is to earn the leadership. Leadership is an action, not a position. Leadership is what you do and how you do it.

The other problem that these kinds of leaders have is that they think they are more important than the people they lead. They tend to devalue the people they lead as they regard them as less important. They almost always place a very high value on holding onto their position—often above everything else they do. They see the position they hold as of more importance than the work they do, the results they produce, the development they offer to their subordinates, and what they generally contribute to their organisation. They think they are not to produce individually but that other people are there to serve their selfish needs. This kind of managerial attitude does not in any way contribute to good working relationships in the workplace. Positional leaders only see a bad attitude in their employees and no weakness in themselves as leaders. They always see their subordinates as threats and obstacles to their progress up the organisational ladder. These kinds of leaders never see the need for personal development or for working well with their juniors. They always see their subordinates as replaceable or interchangeable.

These kinds of leaders tend to create organisational politics that help them to cling to control. They fail to effectively influence because they value their position more than any other thing. This then instils a political environment in the organisation, department, or team they lead. They are always looking for ways to manoeuvre things in the direction they prefer. They think results can only be achieved through the controlling of people. They do not focus on their own individual positive contribution, only on control. They see titles as individual achievements. They build empires. Whatever portion of the budget they receive, they use it to expand the empire and fail to use it to further the organisation's purpose. This then creates a culture of departmental rivalries and silos.

Leaders who base their leadership on control think they have privileges, rights, and entitlements. They do not think they have certain important responsibilities ahead of these rights and entitlements. T. S. Eliot once said, "Half of the harm that is done in this world is due to people who want to feel important. … They don't mean to do the harm. … They are absorbed in the endless struggle to think well of themselves." (Source: Maxwell, 2011)

Positional leaders are self-centred. They do things for the purpose of self-aggrandisement or to make themselves feel or look important. They do things so that their name stands out. Because they fail to influence others through some positive emotional means, they tend to depend on the rights of the position, and arrange things to make it look like they have a sense of entitlement. They often use threats in the workplace as a way of instilling fear in their subordinates. They are clueless about servant leadership. They expect people to serve them instead of the other way around. They cherish their territorial position and regard it as the most important thing at work. You can sense this in how they introduce themselves. Because they depend on the rights and entitlements, they tend to promote those rules and regulations that are favourable to them. Relationships and teamwork are generally not important. These kinds of leaders do not see any need to promote teamwork or create a positive working environment.

Leaders who depend on position can limit everybody else. They end up being isolated because they really do not understand the role of leadership. These leaders also think that when they were made leaders, they were made some sort of king who is meant to oversee everybody from atop some hill. They see themselves as set apart from everybody else. Good leaders know that when the going gets tough, when some people are inclined to give up, they need to walk beside everybody else, helping them to climb the hill. If you think leadership is about climbing the hill ahead of everyone else, you will arrive there alone and find yourself isolated. If you walk side by side with your people, the work environment will become positive for success.

The leaders who regard themselves as kings of the hill become insecure and are easily threatened. As a result, they breed a very negative work environment. Whenever they see people with potential starting to climb, it gets them worried. They fear that their place at the top will be threatened. As a result, they undermine the people who show talent, and they spend most of their time trying to guard their position and keep themselves clearly above and ahead of everyone else. This results in the best people feeling undermined and put down. These talented employees then decide to leave the department or organisation to look for another challenge or hill to climb. Only average or unmotivated people normally stay. And they know their place is at the bottom. This develops an us-versus-them culture, with the positional leader standing alone at the top. Leadership doesn't have to be isolated. People who feel isolated have created a situation that makes them feel that way.

> Remember, when you were made a leader, you weren't given a crown, you were given a responsibility to bring out the best in others. For that, your people need to trust you.
>
> Jack Welsh, former CEO of General Electric

As I have indicated or will indicate in the rest of *Exceptional Leadership*, leadership has a lot to do with influence using some positive humanistic emotional actions such as care, trust, motivation, inspiration, development, and empowerment. If one fails to influence through these means, one tends to resort to depend on position. Once you depend on position, you get noticed and branded as a positional leader. A positional leader lacks most of the soft skills highlighted above. These soft skills are what normally make a leader successful in the long run. Positional leadership is not sustainable in the long run. It either gets a person stuck in one position or gets a person fired in the longer term. It requires a totally new paradigm to change from a positional leader to a more influential leader.

Positional leaders also cause a lot of turnover because of their inferiority complex. People do not quit companies; they quit managers. These leaders get easily threatened by talented subordinates. They develop tactics to frustrate them so they either shape up or ship out. They really do not care when these talented employees leave the organisation. To them, they have succeeded in protecting themselves. They view leadership as survival of the fittest.

Positional leaders cause people below them to be uninspired in the workplace. People below them in turn give them the bare minimum. Because the people you lead are demoralised, they give you their worst performance as opposed to their best performance. It takes positive emotional energy for people to produce at their best. It takes negative emotional energy for people to produce at their worst. Leadership is the determining factor as to the kind of emotional energy that prevails in the workplace.

CHAPTER 4
PERSONAL LEADERSHIP

Leadership really begins when you start noticing yourself as a leader and leading yourself as such. It is in noticing that a leader must possess certain important behaviour traits. Great leaders know that if they cannot lead themselves, they will never be able to lead anyone around them. There are a few things that are important in personal leadership. These include self-awareness, self-management, authenticity, and identifying your personal vision and purpose. Leadership is more about who you are and what you can do. Few things generate as much happiness as knowing that you are fully realising your genius, doing brilliant work, and spending your life in a beautiful way.

And with all the cataclysmic change in our society right now, leadership has become the single most important master skill for success in business. Leadership isn't only something to do at work. We need to practise leadership within every arena in which we operate.

Self-awareness is normally the key to personal excellence and effective leadership. One of the keys to self-awareness is soliciting feedback from those around you and ensuring that you as a leader create a good environment for constructive feedback to be given to you. Many fear-oriented leaders can never receive constructive feedback. People fear for their lives at giving such leaders constructive and honest feedback. They fear the shooting of the messenger who delivers bad news.

Authenticity

Leaders know the importance of being yourself and being original. Robin Sharma indicates that your ability to have an impact and make a great contribution comes more from who you are as a person than from the authority you receive by your placement on some organisational chart. It's never been so important to be trustworthy. It's never been so important to be someone whom others respect. It's never been so important to keep the promises you make to your teammates and customers. And it's never been so essential to be original and authentic. The media, our peers, our bosses, and the world around us pound us relentlessly with messages designed to have us live their values versus our own. There's a huge pull to behave like the majority. But leadership really is about closing your ears to the noisy voices of others so you can more clearly hear the mission and call within yourself. The key is to listen more to your intuition and your conscience. You need to see and importance of the original person you are in terms of your thoughts and feelings. Those who mind your thoughts and feelings do not matter, and those who matter do not mind your thoughts and feelings. You need to develop self-worth and self-confidence to be safe in your own skin. Have faith in yourself, trust your values, discover and live your purpose, and live your life to the fullest.

Being authentic is about being on top in terms of your self-awareness and being proud of who you are. It is about knowing what living your purpose requires and having the courage to live that purpose. It is being your true self in each and every situation rather than when it is convenient. It's about being congruent and consistent so you portray that who you are on the inside is reflected by the way you perform on the outside. And being authentic and true to yourself also means that you meet your potential and work at brilliance—because that's what you truly are.

> To be yourself in a world that is constantly trying to make you something else is the greatest accomplishment.
>
> Ralph Waldo Emerson

A lot of people create problems for themselves by faking who they are or by disguising their true personalities. This then results in a self-created prison. People find it difficult to move out of such a prison when it really matters. To be absolutely fair to yourself is to be extremely committed to living an original and authentic life. This will release you from your self-created prison. You need to stay committed to your purpose as opposed to societal pressures.

We must discover our secret inner power and live guided by it. A lot of people live to impress society or comply with the demands of society instead of living their definite purpose in life in line with their values and original dreams. When you truly understand your life purpose, it reveals to you your values, true desires and hopes, thought habits, talents and potential, habits, and strengths and weaknesses—the things that make us who we truly are. We must learn from our past setbacks and stay focused on our desired destiny. That desired destiny must influence every decision, behaviour, and action you take and every emotion you feel. Once that happens, you will be sure to receive your desired life results.

Fall in love with your vision. Develop the self-confidence to live a life that fulfils your mission and that expresses your highest values. Granted, some people will doubt you and deny you support. Be committed anyway. Be secure in your own skin, and thrive in the face of opposition and criticism. People will try their best to prove you wrong and bring you down. Remain strong and chart the way. Believe in yourself and your God.

Let go of your ego. Please be yourself and no one else. You are beautiful just how you are. A lot of people let societal pressures determine who they are. They always want to beat or compete with the expectations of society. If society is not guided by a moral compass, then this is normally a waste of time. You have to allow your life to be guided by moral principles. Leaders who are guided by moral principles will always be tempted to be humble in an egoistic society.

Effective leaders define their success by what they give instead of by what they get. That not only makes them special in the eyes of everyone around them but also fills them with a great sense of fulfilment and happiness. Think of Nelson Mandela, who had to spend a quarter of his life in prison because it was his mission to fight apartheid and bring freedom to the oppressed black people of South Africa.

Real self-leadership also requires you to work on and renew the four dimensions of yourself, that is the mind, the body, the spirit, and the heart. The renewal of the mind is how you read and acquire new knowledge. The renewal of the body is based on good eating habits and physical exercise. The renewal of the spirit is based on polishing that connection with the highest part of you so that you commit your best years at work to doing deeds that will last beyond your death. The connection with the Creator is also a part of spiritual renewal. The renewal of the heart is a commitment to minimising negative emotions and managing stressful situations.

Our spirit is the most central of all the four dimensions. It ensures that we think the right thoughts, have purified hearts, and take the right actions. Most people don't discover how to live well until they are facing the last few years of their lives. For the majority of their years on earth, they are in a walking coma. They do not really know what their meaning and purpose in life is. It is important to tap into your potential and change your part of the world through the work you do and the person you are becoming. Design your best life, and live to actualise that design. Dig deep into your life by doing all those things that will help you receive the greatest feedback at the end of your life. You need to realise that at birth you were given great talents and precious gifts that need to be put to great use through the life you choose to live.

In the world we live in, success is measured by materialistic accumulation. Society measures you on what you own or what is associated with you. People live lives influenced by ego, chasing job titles, expensive possessions, and financial wealth regardless of how these things come about. We regard these things to mean greatness in life. My experience with people and leadership has shown me that real greatness is determined by how well you affect your fellow human beings. We torture ourselves by gazing into the social mirror. People already know that what makes them great is how well they have an impact on the world around them. The sad truth is that at the end of life, the street sweeper gets buried next to the CEO. And there is no difference in their graves—same size hole, and no first-class site or different route to get in.

Each of us has been blessed with our lives for a particular purpose. We are meant to come into this world to sing a particular song. Allow yourself to sing this song. We have been blessed with unique talents and gifts to sing our life's song. We have to ensure that these talents and gifts are very well used to fulfil our potential.

Each of us has been endowed with the natural power to do some great work and achieve great things. We are meant to manage our habits and our productivity each day to achieve great results. Each one of us has a choice to make to become a good example in life and to live out that good example. You can set good values and then live by those good values.

Each one of us has the potential to set ourselves up to be successful. We can do this by confronting our fears and taking bold risks in life. This will then set us up for great results.

Each one of us has the choice to make to be a master in some craft, meaning that we practise something so well that we excel in that thing.

Everyone in life faces some form of adversity or another. We get knocked down so many times in life. The essence of personal leadership is to ensure that you get up every time you are knocked down. You must be committed to transforming each and every adversity you face into tremendous victory. The Japanese say that if you get knocked down seven times, get up eight times.

I indicated that we are born into this world to serve our Creator. We serve our Creator by serving humanity. We are meant to radically serve other people. Be radical in serving each and every person you meet. You are meant to be a person of ethics, character, empathy, passion, desire, dream, intent, action, and inspiration.

A great person lives his life on his own terms. He sets for himself high life standards and really pushes himself to live by those standards. He does not subscribe to societal influences. He does not allow society to train him for a particular kind of life that fits with society.

A great person always regards herself as a genius, and she always carries herself to the place of her absolute best. She is excited by innovation and is never comfortable with old ways of doing things.

Great people are always inspiring their teammates, customers, and loved ones. They always feel like they are positive impacting the world and leaving a great legacy.

It is important to take charge of both personal leadership and self-management. Personal leadership has a lot to do with having a personal vision, a personal purpose or mission, and personal values. It has to do with having the passion, inspiration, and motivation to fulfil your vision and mission, to live your life in line with your values, and to release your potential. Self-management, on the other hand, has to do with management of the complex variables or factors of our day-to-day lives, including such things as our thoughts, emotions, beliefs, habits, behaviours, and general lifestyle. It has a lot to do with our self-control, self-regulation, and self-discipline. Let us look at a few of self-management responsibilities:

1. Enhance your emotional intelligence.

It is important to understand that your emotions have an impact on the people around you. It's important for everybody to manage their emotions. Nobody likes to spend time with an emotional time bomb who may "go off" at any moment. Emotions are contagious. It is therefore important to be aware of the emotions we feel and to manage those emotions. Negative emotions such as anger, fear, worry, anxiety, guilt, frustration, and disappointment need to be managed so that they do not affect the workplace. A leader's words and actions affect many people around him or her. Good leaders know when to display emotions and when to hide them. Sometimes they show them so that their people can feel what they're feeling. Because leaders see more than others and look ahead of others, they often experience the emotions first. By letting the team know what you're feeling, you're helping them to see what you see.

2. Time management and self-management in light of time.

It is important that each and every hour of your day is spent on things that matter. These should be things that are in line with your meaning and purpose in life. It is important to plan your time well and to manage stress and fatigue. One practice I have seen to be of great value is to work in chunks of time, say, ninety minutes or two hours, and take necessary breaks to refresh. Another is to do thought work in the morning when the mind is still fresh. Yet another is to manage distractions such as emails, text messages, and social media when concentrating on some specific task. The last ritual to practise is the "rule of 5". Through this rule, you ask yourself what are the five most important things you must accomplish today.

3. Prioritise well.

Each and every one of us has things we would like to do. These things must be prioritised according to both urgency and importance. Most leaders are generalists. They know a lot about a lot of things. They often have no choice because they are wearing many hats. But at the same time, the old proverb is true: if you chase two rabbits, both will escape. Leaders have many responsibilities. Therefore they must manage their priorities very well. The things that matter most must never be sacrificed for the things that matter least. The things that are important and urgent must be prioritised ahead of everything else.

4. Manage your energy.

Life is all about energy. There is increasing evidence from science that everything in the universe is comprised of energy. It therefore falls into place that reality is determined by the type of energy frequencies generated by our thoughts. Our internal activities such as our thoughts and emotions are actually actions. And every action has some energy level associated with it. Depending on how energetic the actions, the results produced will also have the same frequency. Energy is the element that is important in every endeavour. So it is important that we channel our energy to those things that matter or to our highest priorities. We also have to ensure we focus our energies on where our passion and purpose lie.

5. Manage your thoughts.

You are what you think. Always ensure that the thoughts you entertain are in line with all the things you want. If you think the things you do not want, that is all you will attract into your life. The thoughts you think are actually like magnets, attracting into your life people and events that harmonise with those thoughts. Our thinking actually sets up a self-fulfilling prophecy. If we think the world is a place of scarcity, then that's the reality we'll end up creating. Thinking is not something that happens to you. It's something that you do. So the key is to ensure that you are doing what is right in your thinking. Train yourself to take charge of your thinking.

6. Manage your vocabulary.

> A powerful agent is the right word. Whenever we come upon one of those intensely right words ... the resulting

effect is physical as well as spiritual and electrically prompt.

Mark Twain

Words are a powerful means of communication. If you want to make someone happy through your communication, you have to find a good selection of words that will make exactly that happen. Also, if you want to make someone unhappy through your communication, you can find a selection of words to do that. Similarly, if you want to get people motivated, you can find a selection of words to do that. Throughout human history, our greatest leaders and thinkers have used the power of words to transform our emotions, to enlist us in their causes, and to shape the course of destiny. Words can create not only emotions but also actions. Therefore in our lives, let us make a good choice in terms of the words we use to express the good intention of following our course.

7. Manage your personal life.

What you do with your personal life matters a lot in your leadership. This includes things like your habits, your values and morals, who you hang around with, and your family life. If your personal life is a mess, then the mess will translate into other aspects of your life. It is also important to manage your personal lifestyle and your general choices in life. Things like diet, fitness, and health are of importance. Spirituality is also important in the modern lives we live. Many of our challenges are spiritual and hence require very strong faith and regular prayer.

CHAPTER 5
GOOD EMPLOYMENT IS KEY

The first responsibility of leadership is about recruiting the right people and placing people in the right places so they can be successful and the organisation can be successful. Recruiting is the first and most important task of creating a winning organisation. Sports teams often serve as a good analogy for the ingredients of organisational success. Former College American Football coach Bobby Bowden was quoted as saying, "If you get the best players and coach them soundly, you're going to win." The most successful coaches in sports are the ones who are best at recruiting the best players. As a leader, you need to know and value your people for who they are and let them work according to their strengths. It is the absolute responsibility of every leader (at any level) to work well with his or her human resources (HR) partners in hiring or recruiting the best people in the labour market for his or her organisation. You don't have to look only for people who will suck up to you. You have to look for people who will work well with you and also who will have the courage to challenge you on issues if required. I always guide my trainees to look for someone who is fitted for the job, but more importantly who demonstrates the right attitude for the job.

Let's consider how some of the most successful CEOs make (or made) hiring decisions:

> I look for three things in hiring people. The first is personal integrity, the second is intelligence, and the third is a high level of energy. But if you do not have the first, the second two don't matter.
>
> Warren Buffett, CEO of Berkshire Hathaway

> Get good people and expect them to perform.
>
> Bill Marriott Jr., CEO of Marriott Corporation

> It doesn't make sense to hire smart people and then tell them what o do; we hire we hire smart people so they tell us what to do.
>
> Steve Jobs, late CEO of Apple

I have seen situations where leaders think they can casually hire someone to work in their organisations because:

- The individual can help them make short-term goals.
- The person is a friend or social mate.
- The person is a relative.

Great leaders know that they have to separate their social connections from their professional work.

The next responsibility of leadership after recruiting the best people is to place those people in the right seats. Successful NBA coach Red Auerbach was asked his secret to success. His answer: "When I first started coaching, people told me to put my best players on the court. But I learned early on that this was not the key to success. It wasn't putting the best players on the court that was going to cause us to win. It was putting the five players on the court who could work together the best. We won championships because we put people together. They weren't always our best players."

John Maxwell says it's not enough just to recruit good players. A leader must understand how those players best fit on the team and then must put them in those places. It all comes from your vision as a leader. You go out and look for the people who will help you achieve that vision and align them well in the organisation.

People who are used to moving fast and flying high are easily frustrated by mediocre leaders who want to hold them back. As a leader, you should always challenge people to move out of their comfort zone, but never out of their strength zone.

Stephen R. Covey says the most crucial activity for any management or leadership team, next to setting up the process for doing strategic pathfinding work, is recruiting, selecting, and positioning people. If a leader fails in this, he or she invites mediocrity into the organisation. To use Jim Collins's language, make sure that you have the right people in the right seats on the right bus. Successful people find their right seats. Successful leaders help their people find the right seats. Sometimes that requires moving people around to find where they will make their greatest contribution. I always say that leadership's first responsibility is to hire the right people. Everything else that follows is dependent on this. If you did not recruit well, then training and development (for example) can become irrelevant. Leaders need to be close to the HR team to ensure that people placement is done in line with long-term visions. There should be no room for shortcuts or for panic or crisis recruitment mode. So it is incumbent upon the leader to ensure that there are systems in place to ensures that those in charge of hiring recruit well, select well, and position people well in the organisation.

I have witnessed some undesirable hiring practices in recent history where HR practitioners would hire only those people willing to give them monetary or romantic favours in exchange for being hired. Great leadership cannot afford to exhibit this kind of behaviour. Leaders need to be certain that the organisation has systems to ensure that the hiring of people is done in line with the strategic criteria of the institution.

Human Behaviour Specialist, Educator, Business Consultant and Author Dr. John Demartini suggests that you always endeavour to hire people whose visions and values overlap with those of the organisation in which they seek employment. Once you have recruited and positioned well, all the other HR principles, such as training and development and performance management, fall into place.

Finding and Keeping the Best Employees

To win the war for talent, leaders need to be able to identify high-potential employees, place them well, develop and empower them, make sure their talents are used, equip them, reassure them of their value, and reward them well so they do not become dissatisfied and leave the company. Leaders also need to be able to listen. Although new employees need strong direction and leaders who can make quick decisions, they expect to be able to challenge leaders' thinking and be treated with respect and dignity. Because of their skills, many employees are in demand and can easily leave to work for a competitor.

Development activities can help companies reduce turnover in two ways: (1) by showing employees that the company is investing in the employees' skill development and (2) by developing managers who will create a positive work environment that makes employees want to come to work and contribute to the company goals. People don't quit organisations; they quit managers. One of the major reasons that good employees leave companies is poor relationships with their managers. Companies need to retain their talented employees or else risk losing their competitive advantage. Development activities can help companies with employee retention by developing managers' skills.

The best companies out there use 360-degree feedback as a way to help develop people skills in their managers of customer contact centres. That is, these companies want their managers to develop skills in communication, creating trust, coaching, and other interpersonal actions that would help the company retain good employees. Managers who score high on the 360-degree assessment normally also ranked high by their employees in providing career development, help, and support. These are the key reasons employees stay with great companies. The 360-degree assessment is linked to a development plan, and each interpersonal skill can be developed through online training. I have come across one company that uses this very well. They set a goal to reduce turnover to 48 per cent. Every branch location that completed the 360-degree assessment met this goal. You cannot ignore the quality of your managers as these are the people who will help retain the best employees and ensure a conducive work climate.

Importance of Effective Recruitment

I consistently tell managers and leaders that to employ the right person is the first and most important responsibility regardless of the type and size of their institution. An effective recruitment and selection process reduces turnover. These processes are geared towards matching up the right person with the right job. Interviews and background checks ensure that the candidate has the right skills and competencies that match the description of the job at hand. This then enables you to employ a candidate who is reliable and will carry out the objectives you have planned for providing quality services and goods to your customers. If you fail at this, you do your company a great disservice.

Recruitment

The recruitment process requires you to ensure that your new hire has the requisite skills and competencies for the job. This is done by analysing the qualifications and experience of the candidate to see how they fare against the job requirements. Will the new hire be able to fulfil his duties straightaway? He might need orientation and minimal training, but he should be able to do the bulk of the work he was hired for. The job advertisement will have outlined the skills relevant to the job. Make sure that your job advert clearly lists all the job requirements such as responsibilities, required education, experience, knowledge, and skills. If you fail to do this, you might end up with a low-quality pool of candidates and wind up with limited choices for filling the open position. When you interview your candidates, ensure that all your questions are geared towards unearthing the necessary capabilities, knowledge, skills, confidence, attitude, and potential of the candidates. Some companies place some importance on the social capabilities of candidates by analysing their behaviour on social media.

Screening and Interview Process

This is one of the most important points in the hiring process, and it must be done in the most thorough of the ways. Bear in mind that nowadays some people are good at preparing to beat the interview by researching the likely interview and practising their answers upfront. The best you can do is to ensure that you have the right team on the interview panel, people who can be trusted to do the job well. The process must really screen the candidates to ensure that there is a right fit between the potential hire and the job. Then the candidates' character, attitude, and behaviours must be tested. Finding the right individual for the job is not just about skills and experience. It is also about determining how you as an employer know you have the right individual and how potential employees know if the job is right for them. The employer needs to establish the overlap between the individual's values, the company values, and the description of the job at hand. If any overlap emerges, then the hiring can move forward.

Everyone has a set of values, or things that are most important to them, which can be determined by observing the actions they take. Values are like fingerprints: no two people have the same set of values, and no one's values are right or wrong. We need a way of identifying the true values of an individual before making a hiring decision, and the individual needs to understand the values of the organisation before taking the job. The employer must be well aware that people are good at preparing for interviews nowadays and that they know how to trick potential employers to get the job they are after. The interviewer must know what the job is and what will be required for a new hire to perform well. Such requirements will include skills, competencies, values, and attitude towards the job.

The interview process also allows you the opportunity to express your company's vision, goals, and needs. It is vital that the interview elicit responses from applicants that can be measured against your expectations for the position. If you don't use the interview to effectively eliminate applicants who don't fit into your company culture, then you might find yourself dealing with turnover, confusion, and disgruntled employees.

Selection

When you choose a candidate based upon the qualifications demonstrated in the résumé the interview, and in the candidate's employment history, background check, values, and personality traits, you will land the best fit for the position. Verification of qualifications, background checks, and psychometric tests are necessary to ensure you hire the right employee. Many organisations these days use psychometric tests to aid in the selection process. The use of psychometric testing gives large and small organisations a competitive edge. Organisations want to know more about job seekers these days, wanting to discover their core competencies through the selection process. Being aware of these desirable core competencies is a good place for you to start so that you can better prepare for and practise psychometric testing such as aptitude tests and personality tests. Certain interesting trends in organisation design highlight that the compatibility between employers and an organisation is becoming more and more important. Employers want a potential hire to share similar characteristics as their organisation, and they use psychometric tests to assess how candidates fit with the organisation and the extent to which the employer and employee will be able to meet each other's needs. Organisations assess aspects such as general intelligence and personality traits through psychometric testing to provide an indication of personal and organisational fit.[1]

Base your decisions about a specific candidate upon specific evidence rather than gut instinct. If you hire people who can do the job instead of people you merely like, you will have higher productivity in your employees and higher quality in your products or services. Your goal in hiring responsible and reliable employees should be to make your business profitable and efficient on a long-term basis. The recruitment and selection process is the time when you not only identify a candidate who has the experience and aptitude to do the job that you are looking to fill, but also when you find someone who shares and endorses your company's core values. The candidate will need to fit well within your company's culture. Your selection and recruitment process should provide you with an employee who adapts and works well with others in your small business.

Failure to recruit and select for the long term can result in high turnover. When you effectively recruit and select the right employee, there is a domino effect. Your new hire will do her job well. Employees will see that you make wise decisions. You will gain respect from your workforce, and you will get higher productivity as a result of that respect. This positive attitude will affect the quality of your products or services, and ultimately your customers' perceptions of your company.[2]

---

[1] Institute of Psychometric Coaching, "Matching Candidates and Jobs Based on Psychometric Tests", https://www.psychometricinstitute.com.au/matching_based_on_psychometric_tests.html, accessed 21 Aug. 2019.

[2] https://www.summitconsulting.co.za/2017/04/13/importance-of-effective-recruitment-selection/.

CHAPTER 6
CREATE AND INSTIL A GREAT VISION

Great leaders know that there is a need to take their organisations to some exciting destiny in the future. They also know the power that lies in having their constituents imagining being part of this exciting and attractive future. A leader needs to create this dream or vision of the future and embrace everybody in it. This vision then needs to dictate the strategies for short-term and long-term success. Leaders create visions by imagining attractive opportunities for the future in line with the organisation's purpose of existence. Once the vision has been determined, it needs to be shared with the rest of the constituents. The leaders need to inspire everybody to adopt the vision as if it's their own. Great leaders always want to achieve great lasting results for the institution. They need to have sustainable results. The organisation must produce now, and it must continue to produce five to ten years into the future. Leaders who only focus on short-term success are weak leaders. So leaders must create great visions and instil those visions into every individual they lead.

We expect a leader to have constituents—or people they lead. If you think you are a leader and there is no one following, then you are not a leader. It is the leader's role to ensure that he has the right people following and to ensure that those people accept the vision as their own. Once leaders are happy with the calibre of constituents they have, they must translate their vision to each constituent. Everyone must be on the same page as far as the vision is concerned. To enlist support, leaders must have intimate knowledge of people's dreams, hopes, aspirations, visions, and values. Leaders forge a unity of purpose by showing constituents how the dream is for the common good. Leaders ignite the flame of passion in others by expressing enthusiasm for a compelling vision of their group. Leaders communicate their passion through vivid language and an expressive style.

An extraordinary leader is one who is able to craft and instil a great vision. Here we are talking about the pictorial representation of the future. People want leaders who are honest, forward-looking, competent, and inspiring. Unless the aspiring leader is forward-looking, people aren't likely to follow her willingly. The trait of being forward-looking for a leader is very important. It demonstrates that the leader is concerned not just about today's problems but also about tomorrow's possibilities. A forward-looking leader is able to envision the future, to gaze across the horizon of time, and to imagine the greater opportunities that exist and that are to come. She sees something up ahead, vague as it might appear from a distance, and she imagines that extraordinary feats are possible and that the ordinary could be transformed into something noble. All enterprises or projects, big or small, begin in the mind's eye through visualisation. They begin with imagination and with the belief that what's merely an image can one day be made real.

Leaders must be concerned not only about short-term performance but also about long-term creation of value. It's an accepted fact of a leader's life. Leaders must first demonstrate their own visions of the future before they can expect to enlist others in a shared vision.

The ability to articulate a clear vision of the future significantly contributes to getting extraordinary things done. Extraordinary leaders have a passion for the institutions they lead, their causes, their techniques, their communities, and something much bigger than themselves and much bigger than all of us. Leaders care about making a difference in the world.

When we think of the best visionaries who had moral authority in the political arena, we think of Martin Luther King, who had a vision for a society where people would not be judged by the colour of their skin but by the content of their character. Even though that vision has not be achieved entirely, I believe it inspired Americans greatly in that they were able to elect Barack Obama as the first black president of the United States of America.

We also think of John F. Kennedy, who had envisioned, among other things, American astronauts landing on the moon. Though he was assassinated early on in his presidency, the vision remained to inspire Americans to land on the moon in 1969.

Of the great visionaries, we also think of Nelson Mandela, who envisioned a multiracial South Africa with people of all races living together in peace in his country. He went on to become the first black president of South Africa in 1994. Again, though he was not able to eliminate apartheid entirely in his single five-year term in office, he left the country almost united. He had used sports to change people's paradigms about their past and to come together in a new rainbow nation.

We also think of Sir Seretse Khama, the first president of my own country, Botswana, who had envisioned to develop a poor country made up of separate tribes with only five kilometres of paved road upon its independence from Great Britain in 1966. Khama's presidency was blessed with the discovery of diamonds in his country, which enabled him to develop his people and his country into a middle-class country together with his predecessor, Sir Quett Ketumile Masire. What I respect most about these two gentlemen is that though diamonds were discovered early on in their presidencies, they did not think of enriching themselves like most African leaders were doing at that time. They were men of character and ethics. They were a totally different breed of African leader who put their country and their people ahead of themselves. Inasmuch as I come entirely from Africa, I have a problem with African leaders. They either lack vision or lack moral authority. This is why Africa, with so many natural resources, fails to develop to First World status, because of greedy leaders who place self-aggrandisement and short-term benefits above the well-being and prosperity of their respective countries. One country that African citizens can learn from in terms of choosing leaders is Singapore.

In the business arena, when think of great visionaries who have inspired many, we think of people like Henry Ford, Andrew Carnegie, Muhammad Yunus, Steve Jobs, Jeff Bezos, Richard Branson, Larry Page, Sergey Brin, and Aliko Dangote—just to name a few. I need to declare up front that I do not know all the great visionaries. If one of your favourites does not appear in this list, it does not mean they are not great. These visionary leaders create great visions that assist in solving some of the world's biggest challenges.

Henry Ford innovated and introduced a simple, strong, reliable car that was affordable for the majority of the people through his company, Ford Motor Company, in an era when the mode of transportation for the majority of people was mainly through walking or using horses, donkeys, streetcars, or trains. Andrew Carnegie was also great in coming up with great visions which pioneered and transformed the US steel industry. Another great visionary was Steve Jobs. Jobs introduced great innovations that transformed the electronics industry, more specifically the mobile phone industry. Steve Jobs shuttered traditional orthodoxies by introducing the smartphone to the market. Jeff Bezos is another great visionary. He founded Amazon.com to bring to the market one of the best online shopping retailers the world has ever seen. Richard Branson, another visionary, introduced Virgin powerful brand of Virgin to the world market. How about Larry Page and Sergey Brin, who founded Google? They organised the world's information and made it universally accessible and useful. Aliko Dangote is one Africa's business visionaries.

He has built a conglomerate that brings a variety of products to the African market. Muhammad Yunus's vision is captured in Stephen R. Covey's book *The 8th Habit*. He is the founder of Grameen Bank, a unique organisation established for the sole purpose of extending microcredit to the poorest of the poor in Bangladesh. When Covey asked Yunus when and how he had gained his vision, the latter said he had no vision to begin with. He simply saw someone in need and tried to fill that need, and then the vision evolved. Muhammad Yunus' vision of a poverty-free world was set in motion with an event that occurred on the streets of Bangladesh.

One might say that I have focused entirely on start-up CEOs. But the same principles apply even if you are a hired CEO or a hired leader in an institution. Actually if you can adopt the attitude that the institution you are leading is a start-up company you founded, you will behave like these great leaders and will provide extraordinary leadership for that institution.

CHAPTER 7

GOOD GOVERNANCE AND ACCOUNTABILITY

As an extraordinary leader, you need to provide accountability. A leader needs to hold himself accountable and to hold everyone he leads accountable. Leaders never lose sight of the fact that good results are all they are after. However, they hold themselves responsible whether the results are good or bad. They are always assertive and candid about how things are going in the organisation. They manage things in a balanced scorecard manner. They regard themselves as the captains of their ship. They have no room to pass the buck, to blame others, or to point fingers.

> Few things can help an individual more than to place responsibility on him, and to let him know that you trust him.
>
> Booker T. Washington

> Remember, when you were made a leader, you weren't given a crown, you were given a responsibility to bring out the best in others. For that, your people need to trust you.
>
> Jack Welsh, former CEO of General Electric

Providing accountability is a behavioural and cultural matter. It is the responsibility of the CEO or top leader to ensure that he or she practises the right behaviours and ensures that the rest of his or her management team (including middle managers) also practise those right behaviours. The culture of any organisation is determined by the top leadership in the organisation. An organisation's culture is a set of behaviours that have become dominant and are tolerated in the organisation. As a responsible leader, you need to occasionally scan the culture of your organisation to check whether the behaviours are still right for the organisation. If the behaviours are not right, they need to be changed. Sometimes this might require you to change your behaviours first before changing those of others. In my book *Become Extraordinary*, I have written about the law of manifestation. This law applies the same to leadership as it does to individuals. The thoughts we tolerate will kick-start a whole chain reaction of things such as emotions, behaviours, and actions that will determine the results of the organisation. So the CEO or top leader must be intentional in getting on top of behavioural and cultural challenges.

Failure in most organisations is the result of the leaders not having the necessary accountability for the business. The culture in a failing organisation is dysfunctional, and the behaviours of the leaders is not conducive for the effectiveness and success of the business. When the CEO does not have the necessary courage and focus to get the executive team and middle management to adopt the necessary behaviours and organisational culture, then the organisation is doomed for failure or mediocre performance.

Peter Drucker is quoted as saying this on culture: "Culture will eat organizational strategy for breakfast." (Source: Maxwell, 2011)

It is the CEO's responsibility to ensure that this does not happen. If the CEO allows his executive team and middle management to operate within the old dysfunctional culture or to exhibit bad behaviours, then he or she cannot expect any extraordinary results. The most important thing the CEO must ensure is that the company's executives understand, address, and stay on top of the challenges they are faced with. Some of the best CEOs I have worked with held weekly business meetings to review and address business challenges. Sometimes these could be long and arduous, but at the end got the business in line. The best CEOs I know ensured that each executive took these meetings seriously. If they were not able to attend these meetings for whatever important reason acceptable to the CEO, they had to ensure that they had a well-informed representative attend in their stead. If any of the executives did not show the necessary seriousness, then they were shown the company's exit door.

The best CEOs will do this without bitterness or malice. They will be dead serious, but they will not be mean in the slightest. And that right there is what every leader of a healthy organisation needs to learn how to do: consistently, persistently, lovingly hold people accountable, not just for hitting their numbers or achieving their goals, but also, first and foremost, for exhibiting the behaviours that the organisation requires.

Great CEOs hold their executives accountable in everything including attending business meetings. In the technological world of today, technology can be a serious distraction in meetings. One CEO I read about was strict on the use of cell phones during executive meetings. If any of the attendees were to use a phone during meetings, he would stop and just look intently at them until they stopped using it and put it away. He created a culture where the executives knew that the first thing they were to do before meetings was to turn off their phones and focus on what was being discussed. Every CEO must have the courage to hold their executives accountable in their work.

Another very important thing that CEOs must do is to eliminate bad politics and behaviour in their organisations. The CEO must start with the executive team and then go on to middle management to ensure he or she squashes out any bad behaviours that contradict what he or she is trying to create. Few CEOs have the courage to do this, and those who neglect to do it implant cancerous behaviours in their organisations. Leaders need to be brutally intolerant of bad behaviours. And once they do that, it will help them to instil a healthy culture in the organisation. Turning the organisation around always starts with creating a new culture and a set of behaviours from the top down.

In our part of the world, we define corporate governance in terms of the King Report and the King Code. This outlines attitude and behaviour that emphasises ethical and effective leadership by anybody given the mandate to govern an institution. This is why the King Report and the King Code is important—it sets out what ethical and effective leadership is. The purpose of King is to:

- Create ethical behaviour and culture in organisations.
- Improve the performance of organisations and increase the value they create.
- Ensure there are adequate and effective processes and controls on how things should be done.
- Build trust between all stakeholders.
- Ensure the organisation has a good reputation.
- Ensure legitimacy.

These are all crucial to building value and creating a better society.[3]

Servant Leadership

Servant leadership is a concept not so common among leaders. Servant leaders see themselves as employees who have been employed to serve the institution to the best of their ability. For those of us who have served in voluntary organisations, the term comes quite naturally. We are used to providing leadership without to nongovernmental organisations without being paid for it. When you are a servant leader, you are a servant first

---

[3] https://www.michalsons.com/focus-areas/information-technology-law/king-report-king-code-on-corporate-governance.

and foremost. A lot of the time, you have a natural feeling of wanting to serve. Most leaders who do not understand the concept of servant leadership think they are there to be served. They see themselves as a rare breed of person who is meant to be served because they have been lucky enough to be put in a leadership position. They see themselves as a leader first as opposed to as a servant first. There is a sharp contrast between the two. The type of leader who is a leader first focuses more on the power she has by virtue of being at the top. This type of leader also focuses on the privileges and material benefits that come with being at the top of the pyramid. The type of leader who is a servant first focuses on sharing power with those she leads. She sees herself as an ordinary person. She focuses on making the lives of those she leads easier so they can perform effectively, and she focuses on helping people, solving problems, developing people, and empowering people so they can perform as highly as possible. Servant leaders focus on the growth and well-being of those they lead. They sacrifice for the least privileged.

Balance of Formal Authority and Moral Authority

We have talked a lot about moral authority and servant leadership. People must not misunderstand this to mean that good leadership is only limited to being kind, respectful, caring, and all the other nice things. These are important of course for the purposes of treating a person like an adult and a human being. But take note that our emphasis on these qualities does not discount the importance of other leadership roles such as managing performance, maintaining disciplined behaviour, and aligning people. Sometimes as a leader you may have to fire someone as a point of last resort. So maintaining a good balance between moral authority and formal authority is quite important.

Ethics and Integrity

It is important for leaders to demonstrate ethical behaviour in order to establish their team's trust in their character. The Harvard Business School asserts that business is a set of norms for what right behaviour looks like in the workplace and how one should navigate the many conflicts that may arise between the interests of stakeholders like customers, workers, management, investors, and the general public. It extends into every part of one's work, intersecting with one's legal responsibilities (to create within the bounds of all laws and regulations) and fiscal responsibilities (to create wealth for the company and profits for the shareholders, for example). As a leader you are a servant of these stakeholders, and therefore you need to demonstrate that all of them can trust that you are running the business according to the highest ethical practices. If you get kickbacks from suppliers and contractors, you are violating the interests of other stakeholders such as investors, workers, customers, and the general public. The world, your country, and the public at large expect that once you are appointed to a leadership role, you are going to serve with utmost professionalism to the best of your ability.

A couple of years ago, ethics used to be the responsibility of the security department, the human resources department, general legal counsel, or senior management. Nowadays it lies within the realm of responsibility of each and every front-line manager's office. In modern business and public governance, ethics is the core responsibility of each manager's office. Each manager holds an obligation to his institution to run it well—whether it is a business, its shareholders, a government institution, the general public, etc. At its simplest level, each manager's ethical position is that they will manage and lead the institution well to ensure that it will be safe and that its resources will be safe. This also entails ethical behaviour and relationships with all employees who work under the manager. Nowadays, there are all sorts of complaints of sexual harassment with some managers tending to abuse their office at the expense of junior officers. There are also issues of favouritism in terms of race, tribalism, nepotism, sexual relationships, etc. In these circumstances, ethics are violated and employee morale and contribution goes down. Employees hold back their best work out of fear and self-protection. The worst and latest ethical violations I have heard of in my own country happen with the recruitment of HR officers who will hire a new employee on condition that the latter will give the former sexual or financial favours for their probation period or longer. This is absolutely unacceptable.

Ethics is at the highest level of self-management. No manager must be tempted to do something that is not right at the expense of the organisation. Each manager must set an example of moral values and standard of conduct. First each manager must ensure that he or she holds himself or herself to a high level of ethical standards by doing the following:

- Managers must task themselves with being courageous and being able to make tough decisions. No leader must bend the rules for popular employees. No leader must turn a blind eye to bad behaviour by some of his or her team members. If a leader has to take an unpopular action against a popular employee, then he or she must have the guts to do that. If the leader has to let a popular employee go, then he or she has to have the courage to take those kind of decisions himself or herself.
- Given that it is human nature to be biased, in each place where you think you are conflicted, it is important to declare interest and then recuse yourself. If you have to make a decision before you recuse yourself, publicly check your decisions for bias. Laura Nash, who has considered business ethics from the perspective of both a consultant and an academic at Harvard Business School, suggests asking questions such as, "How would you define the problem if you were standing on the other side of the fence? Whom could your decision or action injure? Are you confident that your position will be as valid over a long period of time as it seems now? Could you disclose without qualms your decision or action to your boss, your CEO, the board of directors, your family, and society as a whole?"
- If you have to err, then err on the side of protecting the interests of all the most important constituencies of the company—customers, employees, suppliers, and the community at large.

For example, if you have a subordinate who is good at bringing business but who also sexually harasses the people he works with—even people from outside your team—or who arm-twists suppliers for kickbacks, do not turn a blind eye to his behaviour.

Each manager must cascade ethical behaviour to her subordinates. This means creating an ethical culture where individual decisions and actions are scrutinised for ethical behaviour. It means leaders not only talk about ethics but also model ethical behaviour in everything they do. It means creating a culture where people are proactive about testing their decisions against shared moral standards. They don't hide conflicts or ignore them until the conflict becomes more apparent. Ethical thinking is a habit they take pride in. Culture is the way things are done in an organisation. A leader has a large degree of influence over changing the culture by changing individual behaviour. Changing the individual behaviour of individual managers is the best way to manage ethics in an organisation. It all starts with taking individual accountability and then making each manager account for their decisions and actions.

An ethical culture ensures transparency around all issues in the organisation. It ensures that everything is out in the open, including organisational dilemmas and violations. If one of the leaders violates ethics, he is quickly brought to book. No one is above the law. There is consistency in the application of the rules meant to instil ethics. No one has room to break the rules when it is convenient or when it suits them. Everyone develops trust in the rules and systems meant to ensure order.

Leaders who instil an ethical culture ensure open communication from all directions. They empower everyone to be accountable. They make the environment safe for everyone to tell even the most difficult of truths. Leaders must sustain this by making people feel safe to voice the most difficult truths. If the people below you trust that you are sincerely open to these truths, they will feel free to let you know about them—knowing that you are not going to shoot the messenger of the bad news. You must also reward those who communicate the difficult news.

You should acknowledge them publicly and keep their information in confidence as the circumstances demand.

Most companies have codes of ethics that guide employees on how to behave in various circumstances. It is essential that these ethical rules apply to each and every employee, including those at the top and those who are powerful and influential. Good leadership cannot afford to turn a blind eye to some things and apply the rules to other things similar in nature. Leaders need to be consistent in their character.

If you are a good leader, then you always do the right thing, even when no one is looking. You need to be loyal to each and every one of your subordinates as far as ethics is concerned. You must never cover up for your closest cronies and friends. Leaders must have the freedom to break ranks with their closest colleagues if those colleagues become ethical culprits. Your ethical compass must be consistent and straightforward. Leaders must err on the side of disclosure and refuse to cover up. If you are uncertain of whether a matter is an ethical violation, consult with colleagues or experts in the area. Sometimes legal experts may guide in translating the legal implications. Keeping a high ethical standard helps build trust and credibility among the leadership. And trust is a function of both character and competence.

Ethics and Anticorruption

Corruption is one of the greatest enemies of progress in modern times. Corruption destabilises key government institutions, increases inequality, adds significantly to the cost of doing business, and even funds terror. Government leadership that lacks accountability and ethics opens a gateway to corruption and other financial evils of leadership. Running organisations and government institutions is like guiding an elderly blind person on a walk. You have to prevent such a person from tripping over obstacles and pitfalls—hence the need to curb corruption. Corruption is an enemy to economic progress as people are always looking for ways to amass money and enrich themselves. In so doing they lose accountability to those they lead. The problem then becomes systemic as everyone sees the opportunity to loot.

The reason why Africa is so backward economically is because of corruption. Africa has been blessed with resources but is failing in economic growth because its leaders are corrupt. Corruption is rife in Africa because people have created an environment where people who want to steal can do so easily. Africa has institutionalised corruption by creating very weak systems of dealing with the problem. I used to wonder why in some countries, you needed to be economically established before you were allowed to hold a public office. This is to prevent the urge to try to enrich yourself quickly while you are still holding office. However, economics alone cannot get rid of corruption. The good character of those holding positions of leadership is an even greater force.

Corruption distorts decision-making and resource allocation in the interests of a few, harming the fabric of society and destroying trust between citizens and institutions. Openness and transparency are critical to uncovering and tackling corruption in government, companies, and civil society. Corruption and criminal activity thrives under conditions of secrecy. I took a glance at the 2017 Transparency International Corruption Perception Index. Out of the 180 countries, those that are part of the developed world ranked at the top half, and Africa and the rest of the undeveloped world ranked at the bottom half of the index in terms of their economic performance. From the business perspective, large-scale operations such and mining and oil companies are known to lead in corruption activities if the leadership is unethical. Whistle-blowing and protection of whistle-blowers is normally one effective way to stem corruption, coupled with the law taking its course on the culprits. Leaders caught in corrupt activities need to be seriously dealt with to curb and combat corruption.

Declaring of Assets

Some of the experts in anticorruption advise governments, mainly in Africa, of the gap analysis, the difference between international best practices and their existing laws with regard to corruption. These experts indicate that in order for countries to win the battle against corruption, they need to address the issue of impurity, which produces secrecy, thus resulting in corrupt practices. They also indicate that there is a need to come up with a declaration of assets act and a leadership code of conduct, which would basically focus on the values and principles for managing public resources. Established democracies are known across the world for their well-defined asset declaration system as a powerful tool in fighting public sector corruption and abuse of power.

Politicians and civil servants hold substantial power over the allocation of resources in their countries and over the citizens who elect them and who in effect pay their salaries through their tax contributions. The United Nations Convention against Corruption (UNCAC), which has been ratified by 166 countries, requires a legal framework for the asset declaration of government officials. Research shows that an asset declaration open to public scrutiny is a way for citizens to ensure that leaders do not abuse their power for personal gain. Asset declarations are a means to anchor the issue of ethics and integrity in the political classes and should be a part of all codes of conduct.

Money Laundering

Money laundering is very much related to corruption. It is a process of acquiring large amounts of dirty money and pretending as if it came from legitimate sources. There are many leadership ills in the modern era associated with money laundering. Leadership in both government and business organisations need to have their eyes open to possible money laundering issues. Sources of money laundering include corrupt practices, theft, drug trafficking, terrorist activity, and blood diamonds. The acquirer of such ill-gotten money tries to use all sorts of tricks to get this money into mainstream financial institutions as if it had come from a legitimate source.

Illegally earned money needs laundering if a criminal organisation is to use it effectively. True business gets its income in ethical ways, and income earned in such a manner is considered clean money. It is quite difficult to use money that has not been acquired properly. Even some banks are now finding it difficult to do business with money launderers. The repercussions can be quite severe.

There are three main steps in money laundering—placement, layering, and integration. Placement refers to the process of introducing dirty money into financial institutions. Layering is a way of disguising the source of the money. Integration is the act of acquiring the money as if it had come from legitimate sources. Ethical leaders have to have their eyes fully open to all potential money laundering clients in their businesses and government institutions.

Unprofessional Conduct

Jim Collins is famous for his book *Good to Great*. In his second book, he writes about the CEO of a company named Kimberly-Clark. The gentleman was said to have achieved the dramatic turnaround of this company that was not doing well. At the end of his era as CEO, he was asked the secret to his exceptional performance. He simply said, "I never stopped trying to become qualified for the job." Jim continues as follows: "Darwin stands as a classic example of what we came to call a Level 5 leader—an individual who blends extreme personal humility with intense professional will. We found leaders of this type at the helm of every good to great company during the transition era. Like Smith, they were self-effacing individuals who displayed the fierce resolve to do whatever needed to be done to make the company great. Level 5 leaders channel their ego needs away from themselves and into the larger goal of building a great company. It's not that Level 5 leaders have no ego or self-interest. Indeed, they are incredibly ambitious—but their ambition is first and foremost for the institution, not themselves."

CHAPTER 8

RELATIONSHIP MANAGEMENT

Business relationships are important in making your company successful. The real power of building good relationships involves building relational skills—with employees and customers and everyone the business touches. You must have good relationship networks with those within your organisation and with those individuals and groups outside it. Treat these important partnerships as if both partners are equal. Provide wins or benefits for all of them. You can do this by doing the following:

- Recognising what people need and want, and then aiming to create mutual wins for all partners in the relationship.
- Engaging the hearts, minds, emotions, and intellects of the people.
- Establishing, building, and maintaining well-planned and managed relationships, which is fundamental to the success of your business.
- Seeing every person you want to do business with as similar to you in some way in that they want wins of some kind.

One of the greatest things I have learned is that leadership is all about positive relationships. The more you build positive professional relationships, the more it becomes easy to lead other people. When the people in an organisation relate well together, there is no room for silos or interdepartmental rivalries. When relationships are deep, there are no obstacles or barriers that can stand in the way of people working together to produce the best results. These kinds of relationships are created by showing people that you care for them, that you are willing to help them, and that they can trust you in any kind of situation. This produces a positive work environment where everyone likes and respects one another. It is therefore very fair to say people go along with leaders they get along with. Relationships are therefore a major key to success, whether you're trying to sell, coach, teach, lead, or simply navigate the daily tasks of life.

One of the greatest takeaways from the work of Stephen R. Covey is the idea of thinking win-win all the time. If you falter and fail to think win-win, just know that over a long period of time you are not going to have good relationships. An effective life is all about good relationships. Where there is no intentional win-win, trust levels are low. And there is no good relationship without trust. Trust is the magnet of it all. In my book *Become Extraordinary* is a chapter on relationship management. I think it is important here to expand on the thoughts expressed in that chapter.

The required skills begin with the win-win mentality. Then comes the commitment to making all stakeholders happy. How about the need to wow the customer? From the leadership point of view, if you make a commitment to make your employees happy, then they will help you make the customers happy.

An effective team has the ability to work together to achieve a shared goal. In an effective team, team members participate actively, share responsibilities and rewards, and individually contribute their capabilities to the achievement of the team's goal. This kind of team will have members who respect, help, and cooperate with each other and who have high levels of empathy, care, support, and admiration for each other. The leader's responsibility in a team is to build the team spirit, forge positive relationships, and create a unique identity for the team to be proud of. A leader must also ensure that he or she is an active member of the team. An entire chapter on effective teamwork appear later in *Extraordinary Leadership*.

One of the keys to having good working or personal relationships with other people is first to have a good relationship with yourself. This means having immense inner peace. When you have immense inner peace, only then can you have good relationships with other people. This starts with self-awareness. Knowing yourself and being at peace is the key to all other relationships. I have always wondered why Jesus's first statement to his disciples after his resurrection was always "Peace be with you".

How well you relate with others and how well you connect with them is very important if you are to be able to influence them. As indicated earlier, the first thing to do is to have a good relationship with yourself. You have to know and to like yourself. It is a universal human tendency to think you know everybody around you and not to know yourself. Most people can describe one person after another but cannot describe themselves. Even when they think they can describe themselves, they only impart a small version of themselves. Not everybody is gifted with natural self-awareness. The best thing you can do for yourself is to accept your deficiency in self-awareness and become a curious student of yourself. Use all sorts of avenues to improve your self-awareness, including other people's feedback of you. This process will help you to know your strengths and weaknesses in relation to yourself and in relation to other people. Work hard at improving your weaknesses. Pay attention to verbal and nonverbal feedback.

It is crucial to endeavour to know yourself as this could just be the key to relating well with others. I encounter individual clients who indicate that their manager had sent them to one of my trainings only to discover that the manager had a problem relating with himself or herself. These managers send people to courses with the intention of correcting their behaviour, while the manager is the one having a challenge. The problem is compounded if the manager is not open to receiving feedback. Self-exploration is important because if you have a personal challenge that is causing you a problem, you can notice it in time to seek assistance. One of the things I've noticed is that one cannot have peace with other people before one has peace with oneself.

The language you use with other people can be a killer punch that damages relationships. As leaders, we need to know when we uplift relationships and when we tear them down. One time I had a relationship challenge with one of the most important people in my life. I consulted my priest, and he asked me to check my ego and pride before I blamed the other person. It was such great advice as I found traces of egoist defence mechanisms on both sides. Ego can actually force you to neglect other people and focus only on yourself. This is why this matter of caring for other people is the litmus test of positive relationships. Below are a few guiding principles of building good relationships from a leadership perspective:

1. Leadership is all about relationships.

Leaders who want to create good working relationships do not rely on rules to lead people. They don't depend on systems. And they never try to rule with a stick. Instead, they use a personal touch whenever they deal with people. They listen, learn, and then lead. They develop relationships. They have more than an open-door policy—they know the door swings both ways. They go through it and get out among their people to connect. Maxwell (2011) quotes former South West Airlines CEO Herb Kelleher having said, "Leading an organisation is as much about the soul as it is about the systems. Effective leadership finds its source in understanding people. Unless a leader has an awareness of humanity, a sensitivity toward the hopes and aspirations of those he leads, and the capacity to analyse the emotional forces that motivate conduct, he will be unable to produce and be successful regardless of how often other incentives are given."

Another way to say this is that good leaders never take people out of the equation in anything they do. They always take people into account—where they are, what they believe, and what they're feeling.

2. Practise the golden rule.

The golden rule is a basic principle which should always be followed to ensure success in general or in a particular activity. The golden rule is really a moral phenomenon: do unto others what you would like others do unto you. If you do not like something done to you, then do not do it to others. The golden rule is the principle of treating others as one would wish to be treated. It is a maxim that is found in many religions and cultures. The golden rule may be considered the law of reciprocity in some religions, although all religions treat it differently.

3. Strengthen and encourage your team.

Effective results happen or are achieved through the commitment of each and every member of the team. No single individual alone can achieve the results a team can. Actually, effective teams require clear communication, the necessary competence, and commitment from everyone in the team. Leadership then becomes the force that brings it all together. And bear in mind that leadership is a team effort. Leadership is about bringing individual efforts into one collective effort. How frequently do you use the word *we*? Leaders foster collaboration and build trust. This sense of teamwork goes far beyond a few direct reports or close confidants.

Cooperation must move beyond a small group of loyalists. Cooperation must be targeted towards every stakeholder, including those who might have different, independent views. True leaders create a conducive environment for everyone to perform at their best. They give everyone the confidence to be at their best. They empower everyone to own the results. Leadership in modern times is all about inspiration to perform. Command-and-control techniques, using fear and threats, no longer have a place in modern organisations. People learn how to deal with them. They train themselves to deal with or survive the fear induced on them. Effective leaders focus on instilling positive emotions in people.

When leaders focus on the intangibles such as morale and motivation, the tangible results take care of themselves. People need to be trusted to deliver results. When people are trusted and have more discretion, more authority, and more information, they're much more likely to use their energies to produce extraordinary results. Trust to an organisation's leadership is like what oxygen is to life. Development of competence through empowerment is also essential. Valuing and encouraging each individual member adds to their commitment to the team. Encouragement makes each individual member feel strong and causes them to strive to perform at their best. If by mistake or lack of awareness the leader makes someone feel weak, that will affect the person's performance. Leaders must learn to communicate about the best capabilities of their team members as opposed to making them feel weak. If the leader communicates to members that they can do more, it gives them the message that their leader trusts them. It instils them with energy and confidence. It encourages them to employ their best intelligence and energy. Through that process, the constituents grow and learn how best to lead themselves because they observe what works.

4. Motivate and inspire your team.

Make your team like what they do and the results they produce. Leading your team is like taking them to a mountaintop. The journey can be long and difficult. Some members will get tired, some frustrated, and some disenchanted. Some will attempt to give up and abandon the journey. Leaders need to be observant to identify all these types of people so they can encourage them timeously. Leaders must encourage by instilling interest, passion, and energy into everyone. Leaders make others believe in themselves. Encouragement can come in the way of dramatic gestures or simple actions. Leaders need to be proactive and demonstrate appreciation for great contributions. Leaders need to celebrate success with their team members. Individual recognition and group celebration are both key to encouraging employees. It's the leader's most important task to make team members understand the benefits of exhibiting their most desired behaviours. This could be in innovation, enhancing quality, disaster prevention, problem-solving, starting a new product line or service, or creating a new change. When any of these is achieved, celebration needs be made a norm or ritual. It must be authentic, be original, and done in good faith.

5. Build candid communication among team members.

One of the greatest challenges for leaders is to engage in difficult conversations. Creating good working relations means not only being a good friend to your employees but also having to engage in difficult conversations. You can care for people and treat them well but also engage in hard conversations when there is the need. Not everybody will perform well; people will make mistakes; people will have problems—and all these situations will need a leader to put them back on the right path. As a leader, you have to create a history of candid communication, and your subordinates will respect you for it. They will know that you are nice when work requires it, but you are also hard when work requires it.

6. Relate with yourself well.

Self-awareness is an important prerequisite for harmonious relationships. The more you know yourself, the more you know your strengths and shortcomings in relation to others. Who we are determines how we see others. We see the world around us not as it is but as we are. The way we see others is a reflection of self-perception. Our attitudes and beliefs colour not only how we see life but also how we treat others and how we let them treat us. Reality is subjective in a subjective world. Continuous self-exploration, reflection, and acceptance of constructive feedback is important to key relationships. We need to keep on exploring ourselves in various ways in our important journey of self-awareness. The first person we must examine is ourselves. It can be extremely difficult to cope with difficult people, but it can be even more difficult if the most difficult person happens to be you. People who experience relational difficulties are tempted to look at everyone but themselves to explain the problem. However, it's wise to examine yourself first before blaming your problems on someone else. Always ask yourself how your ego and pride have contributed to a particular matter or issue.

One of the most difficult lessons I have learned in the field of relationships is that if one wishes to have peace with other people, one first has to have peace with oneself. If you have some personal hurts, you need to deal with them first before you bring others into your life. People who are hurting can easily hurt other people and can easily be hurt by them. When hurting people lash out, it is in response to what's happening inside of them more than to what's happening around them. As you interact with others, remember this: anytime a person's response is disproportionate to the issue at hand, then the response is a symptom of a deeper issue.

One of the most disruptive emotions is anger. In our day-to-day lives, we get angered by other people, or sometimes we even allow ourselves to be unnecessarily angered. It is important to deal with our anger before we deal with any relational issue. Anger management is key to relationship building and maintenance. As John Maxwell would say, "Never use a hammer to swat a fly off someone's head." Our words can be some of the most dangerous weapons against others in our relationships. We will experience conflicts in our lives. We must always make a conscious effort to choose opportune times to engage in these conflicts, and we must monitor both our tone and body language when expressing disagreements. In relationships, having a winsome attitude is more important than winning arguments.

In any relationship, you should be a person who builds up other people. Do not be a person who tears people down. People value themselves, and they do not want to be demeaned or torn apart. So in all our leadership relationships, our strategy must be to lift people up and not to tear people down. Within every relationship lies an opportunity to build up or tear down. Leaders seize the opportunity to add value to those closest to them.

Great leaders always aim for something bigger than themselves. Their self-interests are always subordinated to something much bigger than themselves. Great leaders watch to ensure that their personal egos do not get ahead of organisational interests. Egos can be positive if they are more inclined towards organisational contribution and achievement. They can be more negative if they are inclined towards self-aggrandisement and self-promotion. The entire population of the world, with one minor exception, is composed of others. One of the greatest qualities of a human being when it comes to relationships is to be kind and humble regardless of what the other person has done to you. My melancholic temperament has always placed me in a ready mode to verbally strike out against the other person I supposed to have offended me. In some situations I find myself regretting what I actually said to the other person. I need to right these wrongs to keep in line with the protection of my own peace of mind and the positive maintenance of the relationship with the other person.

In my book *Become Extraordinary*, I have written about personality types and how they affect our interactions with others. Being choleric and melancholic as a personality type can close you down to learning from other people. We should approach other people with the desire to learn from them. One of the main determining factors in relationships with other people is how we engage them in life matters. If you gauge or rank someone lowly, they will resist relating well with you. People also want to be regarded as individuals who add value. John Maxwell always says to treat everybody as a ten. This implies believing in them as if they have the potential to be developed to a ten on a scale of one to ten.

We have said a lot about caring for people in relationships. Although you might be a caring person, let your caring not hinder you from confronting people when there is the need. Perhaps there are issues of nonperformance that might require you to confront an individual, so you must not shy away from doing so. You must create a good balance between caring for people and confronting them. Sometimes there will be conflict. You cannot afford to avoid conflict in a leadership situation. The ability to manage your emotions and respond appropriately to the emotions of others determines your success in tense situations. When seeking a resolution, always try to remove your emotions from the matter at hand. Always try to be as calm as possible, even when the matter is emotional.

We have talked a lot about character as an important component of leadership. As a leader, you have to ensure that you have a character that people can trust. One of the important character traits that leads to good relationships is trust. It is my greatest belief that trust is earned and not just easily or simply received. For you to earn trust from the people around you, you have to do a good job of ensuring that you are person of trustworthiness. You cannot separate trust from trustworthiness. If you are a person who is fond of doing things that lack trustworthiness, then people will have every right not to trust you. But unfortunately trust is the foundation of all relationships.

In my emotional intelligence courses, I always emphasise emotional self-awareness and emotional social awareness. If you are strong in these two aspects, you will always have strength in dealing with your most important relationships. If your emotional well-being is low, you will have to work on controlling your emotions so that they do not affect your relationships. If the other person's emotional well-being is low, take responsibility to assist them in dealing with their emotional challenge, again so that it does not have an adverse effect on their relationships.

Leadership must be situational all the time. Some situations will be more complex than others. Under no circumstances should a situation be more important than the relationship. It is more rewarding to resolve a situation than to dissolve a relationship. If you're not careful, you might magnify a simple quarrel to the point where it distorts your picture of the entire relationship. Keep petty disagreements in perspective, and refuse to let them erode your relational bond with a friend.

CHAPTER 9

EXERCISE GOOD HUMAN RESOURCES PRINCIPLES

Great leaders know that the bulk of their responsibility is about managing and leading the human resources. They endeavour to ensure they employ a smart human resources management (HRM) team that will help provide great leadership to the human resources. You will notice that to provide leadership for human resources, a leader needs to be tuned in to people skills or what other people would call soft skills. As a good leader, if you do not have the requisite people skills, you may initially use a smart HRM team to build those skills. Once you have a competent HRM team, you must build your own soft skills so that there is harmony with your team. There is no shortcut to achieving important things. What is important is that you must build a competent HRM team as opposed to an incompetent and mediocre one. It is also important at the outset to hire a competent leader or leaders. I have always seen that a good leader paired with a professionally competent and smart HRM team produces good results for the organisation.

A good balance is very rare these days in most organisations. It is either that you see a mediocre leader with a good HRM team or a good leader with a mediocre HRM team. The latter is better because the good leader will notice that his team is not good enough and replace them. The former is not good because the good team will be frustrated by their mediocre leader unless they have a strong influence upward. All the great things I have written and said about extraordinary leadership will be irrelevant if you do not have great leadership who ensure the application of good HR principles—good recruitment and selection, relationship building, people development, performance management, promotions and succession, rewards and remuneration systems, job analysis and design, etc.

If you fail in most of these areas, your leadership will be ineffective. Indeed it will be a nightmare. Most of the foregoing things are what holds the organisation together and keeps it in good shape. I have seen organisations that conduct climate surveys every so often and receive consistently negative results. My assertion is that the problem with those organisations is ineffective leadership that fails in most of these key areas. If a climate survey receives a negative result, it will take strong leadership to turn that result into a positive one. The reason why most organisations keep getting negative results on their organisational surveys is that they have weak leadership.

The key role that HRM plays is to determine the survival, effectiveness, and competitiveness of the business and organisation. Competitiveness refers to a company's ability to maintain and gain market share in its particular area of industry. Great human resources management practices help support the company's business strategy and provide services to customers. The value of a product or service is determined by its quality and how closely it fits with customer needs. Products and services are produced by the employees or human resources of the organisation. Great organisations know that if they are to wow their customers and deliver great products and services, they must first treat their employees very well. And that implies being on top of their human resources principles as outlined in this chapter.

Competitiveness is related to company effectiveness, which is determined by whether or not the company satisfies the needs of stakeholders (groups affected by business practices). Important stakeholders include stockholders, who want a return on their investment; customers, who want a high-quality product or service; and employees, who desire interesting work, reasonable treatment, and compensation for their services. The community, which wants the company to contribute to community activities and projects and also minimise pollution of the environment, is also an important stakeholder. Companies that do not meet stakeholders' needs are unlikely to have a competitive advantage over other firms in their industry, let alone survive.

Biniam Kassa once asserted, "Human Resources management (HRM) refers to the policies, practices and systems that influence employees' behaviour, attitudes, and performance. Many companies refer to HRM as involving 'people practices'. The figure below emphasizes that there are several HRM practices. The strategy underlying these practices needs to be considered to maximize their influence on company performance. As the figure shows, HRM practices include analyzing and designing work, determining human resources needs (HR planning), attracting potential employees (recruiting), choosing employees (selection), teaching employees how to perform their jobs and preparing them for the future (training and development), rewarding employees (compensation), evaluating their performance (performance management), and creating a positive work environment (employee relations)."

The discussion at this chapter's opening highlight how effective HRM practices support business goals and objectives. That is, effective HRM practices are strategic! Effective HRM has been shown to enhance company performance by contributing to employee and customer satisfaction, innovation, and productivity, and the development of a favourable reputation in the firm's community. The potential role of HRM in company performance has only recently been recognised. Smart leaders take advantage of these practices in addition to their other responsibilities of leading well. The CEO needs to fully embrace these principles and also ensure that her senior and middle management teams embrace them. Anybody who violates them needs to be fired. The more the leaders can do great work in these aspects, the better the climate within the organisation. The more the leadership violates the principles of these aspects, the more negative the organisation's climate will be.

One source of failure in many organisations is when the leader causes or allows violation of these HRM principles. If you start hiring people who do not have the necessary prerequisites, for example qualifications, competence, and fit for the job, then the rest of the organisation is going to notice, and it is going to cause a problem in the organisation. In one of the organisations I was consulting for, people told me with conviction that the HR manager was engaging in preferential hiring. "He is hiring only people from his tribe." This was so engrained that people were always curious to know where the newcomer originated from to prove their conviction. Any CEO or senior manager who allows this to happen is sleeping on the job. There must be no discrimination. The only hiring criteria used should be qualifications, competence, and fit for the job. It must be the manager's intention to hire the best people from the labour market.

Another violation of HRM principles is to promote people who are not competent among the workforce. This is very common in most organisations I have dealt with. The situation becomes even worse if the top leader is a control freak as he or she will always be looking for people he or she can control, as opposed to looking for people who can assist him or her in leading the organisation well with great use of diversity. Only incompetent leaders can be controlled. Competent leaders want to be allowed to lead in their own ways to deliver the desired results.

The other thorny issue that I have observed in most organisations is performance management. If this is not done right, it can cause major climate issues in an organisation. This is so because performance management is always connected with important employee issues such as promotions, rewards, and remuneration. The longer you fail to handle performance management, the more susceptible you will be to causing "cancer" in your organisation. The more you fail to handle this one aspect, the more you will lose control in most other areas. And this will cause a loss of morale in your organisation. This is why as a leader you need to pay attention to these intangible issues of business. The more these intangibles are in order, the more the tangibles will take care of themselves. I include a whole chapter on performance management to help you perform this role very well.

The other unethical thing I have seen most leaders engage in or allow is the having of intimate relationships with juniors. Again, once you venture in this kind of area, you start losing control over an array of other matters in your organisation. By indulging in an act of this nature, you lose respect, trust, and many of the important things mentioned earlier. Issues around perceived favouritism and preferential treatment are going to be an everyday refrain. People will be watching your every step to see where they can castigate you.

It is very important for a leader never to violate the psychological contract developed between the organisation and the employee. The psychological contract is the unwritten set of expectations of the employment relationship between the employer and the employee. It is an intangible component of employment that is distinct from the formal documents that make up the employment contract. It was quite common for leaders and managers to be negligent with regard to the psychological contract and focus only on the employment contract. Leaders who do this do so at their own peril. The psychological contract involves perceived relationship expectations between the employee and the employer. When a new employee is hired, obviously some expectations develop between the two parties. These expectations cannot be ignored. There might have been promises of potential progression or promotion, salary increase, personal development, and so forth, and these may form part of the psychological contract. A good employer cannot ignore or neglect these perceived expectations. Both parties need to be alert to any potential deviation of the psychological contract. Constant communication about work and associated concerns is important. This communication must not be left to HR personnel but remains the sole responsibility of the employee's superior.

Job Analysis and Design

Another important HR principle not to be taken lightly is job analysis and design. Organisations are not static. They evolve over time because they grow. An organisation may start out as small, but over a long period of time the overall mission and objectives of the institution may become far too large for any single person or a few people to accomplish. Consequently, groups of people perform specific functions or tasks, providing the mechanisms for coordinating and linking the various activities that are necessary for success. These activities unite to form jobs that the organisation is built upon. Jobs can be broken down into components and arranged in a hierarchy of work activities. Job analysis must always be conducted according to a systematic process. Job analysis answers a number of important questions, as follows:

- What knowledge, skills, and abilities (KSAs) does the job holder need?
- What kinds of behaviours are needed to perform the job?
- What traits and experience does the job holder require?
- What machines and special equipment must be used?
- How much supervision is necessary?
- Under what working conditions should this job be performed?
- With whom does the job holder interact?
- How much time is taken to complete important tasks?
- What are the performance expectations for this job?
- How can the information acquired by the job analysis be used in the employee's development?

Job design is a process of designing how work will be performed and the tasks that are required in a given job. Job design refers to changing the tasks or the way work is performed in an existing job. To effectively design jobs, one must thoroughly understand the job as it exists (through job analysis) and its place in the larger work unit's workflow process (workflow analysis). By having detailed knowledge of the tasks performed by the work unit and on the job, a manager has many alternative ways to design a job.[4]

Most of what management and leadership is about is harnessing human resources principles because work is all about dealing with people. Even if you have to discipline someone, discipline them in the right manner according to procedures they are well aware of. Trampling over human resources principles will make your work much more difficult. One of the most common leadership mistakes we make is not to hire the most suitable employees and instead put an unprepared person in the thick of things. From then on we treat this employee very badly because he is not up to the job. We do not even give him a good enough orientation to do the job. We treat him very badly— as a thing in the knowledge worker age. We do not appreciate his contribution. You may give someone a three-month probation and then extend it for no apparent reason. You may not give them enough supportive measures, including training and development, to help them and guide them in their work. You may not even mentor new employees, leaving them confused. You may not give them credit when they deserve it, or even if you do give it, you don't give it in good faith.

Job design measurement is very important to making sure you turn create a proper job description so that the employee knows what the boundaries of her job are. She also will know exactly what she has been employed to do. Job measurement also helps in workforce planning by letting you know how many employees you need. It is very painful for employees to overload them with work because of poor job design and measurement. It is important to have good job descriptions with clear key performance indicators (KPIs). Good job design and measurement guides other important principles like work pay or remuneration and promotions.

---

[4] http://www.whatishumanresource.com/job-design.

Managers must recognise the fact that there are laws regulating hours of work. Leaders need to know and accept that there is life outside work. This way, they can assist employees in achieving an effective work–life balance. A manager cannot just work an employee more hours than are legally allowed. Hours of work must comply with labour laws. An employer or the representative of an employer cannot act above the law. If there is need for training on this important aspect, it must be delivered to those responsible for this compliance. In addition to respecting the legal requirements, leaders must also exhibit humane and ethical behaviour. Good conflict resolution skills are very important in the workplace. Leaders, managers, and supervisors need to equip themselves with good leadership qualities such as motivation, empowerment, assertive communication, and empathetic listening.

Workforce Planning

It is important for managers to recognise that a well-mannered, talented employee is an asset to the company. Such an employee must be treated in a way that ensures he performs, is empowered, grows, develops, contributes, and progresses. Any violation of these principles causes animosity and dissatisfaction. This often leads to premature separation with the company or even unfair dismissals, which end up costing the company a great deal. I have seen situations where an employee is dismissed for what is termed "insubordination", only to find that it was just a difference of opinion. This often arises from incompetent leadership that is poor on employee relations. You cannot afford to confuse an objective difference of opinion with insubordination. These kind of behaviours will shutter an employee's psychological contract to the point of no return.

When organisations become more global, workforce planning becomes more important and more complex. Most companies nowadays are facing serious global challenges. As R. A. Noe et al. put it, companies are finding that in order to survive, they must establish themselves as forces to reckon with in the global marketplace. They go on to say that to compete in the global marketplace, businesses must understand cultural differences and invest in human resources. As companies become global, one of the daunting tasks facing human resources management is workforce planning. As different markets perceive products and services differently, it is always difficult to plan which skills and competencies are required where. The markets are also dynamic, and therefore issues of sustainability arise. Sullivan explains that workforce planning is a systematic, fully integrated organisational process that involves proactively planning ahead to avoid talent surpluses or shortages.[5]

Global companies may have to outsource some of their jobs based on skills rationalisation. This becomes a challenge for many companies as not every employee may be willing to go and work in another country. For employees with families, they may find it difficult to relocate to a foreign place, basing their decision on the education of their children and also on the change of culture that they will have to experience. If certain sections of the workforce are not willing to go abroad, this becomes a huge hiccup for workforce planning as certain jobs have to be exported nevertheless.

Sometimes companies face cultural constraints as their employees working in foreign countries still have to work effectively to meet the demand of the local markets in which they operate. It is also important that those in management and leadership positions to be aligned with the different cultures that they operate in so as to be able to maintain the effectiveness of the local workforce. Noe et al cites an article by (Patton, 2004: 34–38) illustrates that PricewaterhouseCoopers became very smart in this area by developing its Genesis Park global leadership programme. The programme "is designed to rid any cultural biases that participants may have about team work and creative thinking and build them into an effective multinational team who can help solve in-house or client problems".

---

[5] 10SR journals. Dr. John Sullivan (November, 2002: Work Planning: Why to start now. pp 46 – 50) accessed 11 November 2019

In some countries, a globalised company may face stiff competition related to labour costs. Chinese companies are winning this competition. This becomes a challenge when the communities with cheap labour do not necessarily have workers with the required level of skill. To maintain the quality of the products and services, companies may have to resort to a more expensive workforce or opt for training an unskilled workforce. This might not be easily or readily achieved in the short term, which then demands that companies be very sharp in determining their future labour surpluses and shortages. A good balance of cheap labour and the right level of skill becomes a critical factor when trying to gain or maintain a competitive advantage. It is also important to have the right size workforce to cope with varying demands of production to avoid a labour surplus or shortage. Because of the turbulent marketplace and the varying demand for products and services, it is very difficult to forecast labour requirements. This calls for highly qualified human resources professionals who can do high-quality human resources planning. They will be able to use qualitative and quantitative forecasting techniques to align the human resources requirements with the organisational strategy.

The other major challenge companies face is a war for talent. Companies which offer better packages may poach talented employees from their competitors. Companies may respond to this by competing on remuneration and other benefits or else face the daunting task of training and retraining their workforce for survival. Another problem facing globalised organisations is taking an inventory of the organisation's skills. Nel et al. indicate that the United Nations Office of Human Resources did an online survey of skills and experience, setting up a new skills inventory. This skills inventory was then to be used in workforce planning to provide a clear analysis of what skills were being lost and to help the UN with future recruitment. Another, secondary problem may be the availability of technology to enable an organisation to forecast labour surpluses and shortages as well as the availability of skilled workers. Organisations need to embrace the right kind of technology to be able to compete in the globalised world. The availability of relevant human resources management information systems is of paramount importance. With ever-changing technology, information, and knowledge work, it is difficult to predict future demands in specific job categories or skill areas.

In the globalised marketplace, whatever workforce planning strategies organisations use must avoid human suffering, as this may create unrest in those who remain in the organisation and lead to unwanted turnover as people seek job security. Organisations need to have a great vision for the training and retraining of employees. Exposure to other operations to prepare the workforce for international assignments is important.

Recruitment and Staffing

One important leadership responsibility is to staff the organisation and align the workforce with the business strategy. A staffing strategy is a technique used by an organisation to place the right person in the right position. These strategies are categorised as either internal or external (Nel et al.). Here I will compare and evaluate staffing strategies I have observed that are likely to be at the disposal of managers in Southern Africa.

As vacancies are created in organisations, Southern African managers, like most managers worldwide, are faced with the task of filling these vacancies. The strategies available to managers for staffing vacant positions are categorised as either internal or external. The application of these strategies is made much easier if there has been good workforce planning.

External strategies of filling vacant positions can be applied when there is a shortage of skills from the employees already in the organisation. They may also be applied if diversity and new ideas from outside are required. It is quite important that good recruitment decisions are made in order for the organisation to benefit from potential diversity and new elements of creativity. It is quite possible that an employee will be recruited from outside the organisation, only to find that that employee's performance does not meet expectations. If this employee does not outclass the employees already in the organisation, his hiring might be a demoralising fact to those who think they should have been considered for the position. If the employee does outclass those he finds in the organisation, his hiring may not be questioned or might boost the morale of all his new colleagues. The organisation will also greatly benefit from the levels of diversity and creativity, the new perspective, and the productivity that will be brought into the organisation.

However, in some countries such as South Africa, external strategies might have to be employed because of affirmative action, for example Black Economic Empowerment. This has its advantages and disadvantages. The advantage is that it creates opportunities for previously discriminated-against groups of people. The disadvantage is that it may sacrifice quality, especially where there is a shortage of skills. It also calls for managers to make the best recruitment decisions in the interest of giving the organisation a competitive advantage and not just for PR purposes.

There are several strategies that may be used to staff internally. One of these is to promote those employees with good performance records. This strategy encourages a spirit of good performance in the people who position themselves for development and performance for superior positions. Some countries such as Botswana have localisation policies that encourage senior positions (that have been held by expatriates) to be given to deserving locals at the end of the expatriates' contracts. This practice is positive in that it encourages a spirit of high performance in those ambitious locals eyeing those positions. However, the practice may be counterproductive if the locals who do get promoted do not meet the right levels of competency and productivity.

Another strategy of staffing is to transfer employees within an organisation. Transfer is good for the employee in that it brings her new challenges and opportunities for growth. It is also good for the organisation in that there is an opportunity for new ideas and a new level of motivation from the employee in the new position. The arrival of the new employee also has the potential to motivate and empower her new colleagues.

The last strategy of staffing is demotion, where an employee is placed in a position of a lower grade than that which he already holds. Nel et al. indicate that this happens when an employee is punished for an offence or is redeployed. Demotion can be an objective strategy to place a person in the right position if it is noticed that the employee was promoted but exhibits utmost incompetence and it is realised that there will be no training and development that will engender competence in the short term. This normally happens in positions of where a person is required to make critical decisions. This kind of decision might be painful for the employee but might be good for the organisation for the purposes of competitive advantage.

Bearing in mind issues such as unemployment, skills shortages, and global competition, the foregoing are some of the strategies that I think are situationally ideal for countries such as Botswana.

In Botswana, a good proportion of the population is unemployed. The reason for much of this unemployment is, of course, a lack of skill. However, in the last decade there has been a constant increase in the number of qualified professionals in various disciplines in both the private and public sectors. In the past ten to twenty years, the country has seen a constant increase in business start-ups as it has grown from a poor to a middle-class economy. There are a number of foreign companies that outsource to Botswana. For most of these companies, it would be best if they were to bring some of their internal employees for the more specialised jobs and hire locals for the less specialised jobs.

In the past decade, the mining sector has seen tremendous growth, becoming the second major employer after government. The mining sector continues to grow with the opening up of new mines in several parts of the country. The mining sector, being a complex industry, requires a high level of engineering skills, but Botswana faced a shortage of appropriate skills in engineering when the mines were first opened. Faced with this scenario, most companies were left with no choice but to seek staff externally, even crossing international borders to find the much-needed engineering skills. Most companies revised their remuneration packages to make themselves able to attract expatriates to their ranks. This helped many of these companies to compete for high levels of skills internationally, enabling them to become well-positioned for competing globally.

As the country enjoyed this period of development, many locals graduated from universities with engineering and business degrees. This then flooded the labour market with young people with no experience. Many organisations are now absorbing these young graduates as learner officials for future promotions into more senior positions. Organisations see this as a way of relieving themselves of the huge recruitment costs of employing expatriates. This practice also helps the organisations to align to the localisation policy that some African governments introduced a couple of years ago. Some of the organisations send their local employees to their sister operations or partners outside the country to gain new experience and bring back new levels of skills for a competitive advantage. Organisations with more than one operation transfer employees around their operations to balance their skills requirements. This is important for these operations in that it brings in new skills and perspectives. High performers are promoted to senior positions, and this has a cascade effect on the spirit of high performance in the organisation as people look towards aspired promotions.

In my country, Botswana, some of the mining organisations recruit top high school leavers and sponsor them for various technical courses. Upon completion they absorb them as learner officials in preparation for taking up managerial positions down the line. This practice, though expensive for smaller companies, has proved a lifeline for big mining companies. The small companies compete with the big ones for those employees whom they can entice with better short-term packages. The manufacturing industry is very small in most countries in Africa, but the staffing trends are similar to those of the mining sector. These businesses recruit a few expatriates if they have many of the requisite skills. These employees are then leveraged to train and develop young, inexperienced, lower-skilled employees in the company for future internal staffing.

It is not easy to prescribe a certain staffing strategy for Botswana. This is mainly because country has experienced fast development since independence. Almost everything in the business sector has been dynamic. The country caught up with the industrial model of businesses and in a very short spell of time had to transform and use the information and knowledge worker model.

Remuneration and Job Pay

One of the most important jobs of the HRM side of an organisation is to adopt a good pay system. Although there are a number of innovative pay systems available, many organisations believe that the traditional job-based pay system is still the best choice. A number of organisations use the job-based pay model to decide pay structure for their employees. The job-based pay model can use internal job evaluation methods as well as market surveys of other industry competitors.

A job evaluation process assumes that there are certain job factors that need to be quantified and qualified, and these factors are then used in making compensation decisions. A job evaluation process will normally begin with job analysis which brings such things as job descriptions and job specifications. These two tasks require an enormous amount of experience and competence in the industry for which jobs are evaluated and special HR expertise specific to job analysis and evaluation.

After the analysis of jobs, the job evaluation process will then determine what Nel et al. call compensable factors. These are factors that are taken to be important and necessary for acceptable job performance and contribution towards the organisational goals. These factors may vary from industry to industry, but some general examples are complexity of the job, decision-making, judgement to be made, planning, reasoning, know-how, and supervision. Currently in Southern Africa there are three main types of evaluation techniques in use according to Nel et al. (2003) asserts "In South Africa, popular forms of the factor comparison and points job evaluation methods are the Patterson method – based on decision-making; Hay method – based on factors such as know-how, problem-solving, and accountability; and Peromnes method – based on the eight factors of problem-solving, consequences of judgement, pressure of work, knowledge required, job impact, educational qualifications, training, and experience"

It must be noted that despite the fact that one or another of these methods is widely adopted by organisations worldwide, they may remain very subjective in the way they are applied. The fact that they are based on the opinions of people perceived to have the right kind of competence and HR expertise leaves room for subjectivity, and therefore the methods might vary from organisation to organisation. To get around the subjectivity, Nel et al. (2003) assets "Because it is impossible for one person to have a compressive knowledge of all jobs in an organisation, especially in a large company, a trained job evaluation committee usually carries out the factor comparison and points methods of job evaluation. The committee members should have an adequate knowledge of all work areas in the organisation, and should have received basic training in the way that job evaluation is carried out." Nel et al. (2003) propose that an effective job evaluation committee must consist of the departmental head of the section in which the job to be evaluated is performed, the departmental head of another, neutral section of the organisation, a trade union representative, and a human resources representative. In most cases, this normally seems a complementary team for the process, but the choice of people must be made carefully. After doing department-wide job evaluations, organisations may sometimes do company-wide evaluations, which can get complex because in this case jobs are being compared with others across disciplines. Noe et al. indicate that a point factor system may be used to score the compensable facets. Evaluators give scores to various compensable factors and then apply weights based on each factor's relative importance. The weight can be based on expert judgements or on empirical methods based on the importance of these factors in the labour market.

Once the evaluation of various jobs has been done, the respective values of the jobs can be used to rank the jobs and slot them in a hierarchy that determines which jobs are deemed important for the achievement of the organisational goals. This is how departments in organisations are built up, by comparing the value of one job with other jobs. Once the hierarchy has been determined, job grades or bands are created. Jobs that are deemed to have relatively the same level of importance are put on the same grade or band. The job-based pay model then concludes by paying jobs of the same grade similarly.

Job-based pay may require organisations to conduct a market survey in order to benchmark the wages and salaries of top talent for purposes of retaining that talent. Either the organisation itself may do the market survey, or it may hire a consultant to conduct the survey. Whatever the case may be, it is normally a complex task and may result in subjective results. In the gathering of data for the market survey, the organisation identifies key jobs depending on whether the jobs are core jobs of the industry concerned, whether the jobs require scarce skills, whether the jobs are specialised and unique, and more important in today's world whether the jobs are knowledge-based. In doing this task, the organisation will have to choose the organisations with which to compare itself and the jobs to be compared by following the foregoing criteria. The organisation may compare key jobs to see how other industry competitors are paying those jobs. After comparing these key jobs, the organisation makes decisions on how to pay these jobs based on the market comparison. Most organisations use the data of key jobs comparison to determine the pay policy line. The pay policy line is drawn by plotting the market survey salary data against the job evaluation points. By extrapolating the results and using the job evaluation points of non-key jobs (that were not compared in the market survey), the relative salaries of these jobs can be determined. However, Noe et al. indicate that there may be other factors such as whether many people in the labour supply can do the job being compared, which may cause conflicts between the market survey and the job evaluations. Organisations may deal with this problem by striking a good balance between attracting desirable candidates for its jobs and keeping labour costs within control. But under normal circumstances, these two methods beef up each other.

Another way of using the market survey is to determine the pay range by establishing the minimum and maximum pay for specific jobs. After establishing the range, the organisation may come up with the minimum, midpoint, and maximum of the pay range. Once this is established, the organisation then decides to pay its jobs below the fiftieth percentile or above the fiftieth percentile, whatever the case may be. These kinds of decisions may be based on overall labour costs of the organisation or on the nature of the business of the organisation. This kind of pay system normally works well for leading industry organisations when the survey data are representative of the market situation. Like all the foregoing methods, the effectiveness of this compensation system depends on the accuracy of the survey information and the manipulation techniques used to determine the unknowns.

Despite the fact that job-based pay structures have proven to be the most widely used pay system, they may also have some negative effects on the organisation. Noe et al. highlight these points as follows:

- A job-based pay structure may encourage bureaucracy.
- The hierarchical nature of the structure may encourage top-down decision-making and information flow as well as a status differential. However, organisations that exercise moral authority as opposed to formal authority may not have this problem.

- The bureaucracy involved with the job evaluation process and determination of job descriptions may be a barrier to doing a good job with this process.
- Job-based pay may not reward certain desired behaviours, especially in our knowledge worker era.
- Emphasis on job levels and the status differential encourages promotion seeking within the organisation.

The problems of the hierarchical nature of job-based pay systems may be minimised by delayering or broadbanding. This process reduces the number of job levels, which has a positive effect on the bureaucracy, and reduces formal authority.

Another way of dealing with the problems with job-based pay is to pay for the skill, knowledge, and competence of the person. This will increasingly be seen in knowledge worker organisations.

Following the foregoing discussions, it will be noted that the job-based pay system is seen more in hierarchical organisations that have departments and divisions.

Spirituality and Wellness

The last thing I would like to touch on is the importance of spirituality and wellness programmes for staff and how these can contribute to a holistic approach to healthcare in the workplace.

Nel et al. indicate that emphasising spirituality at work attempts to make corporations friendlier and leads them to develop a more creative environment by tapping into the spiritual side of employees. Today's management and leadership needs to tap into the spiritual side of employees or enhance employees' spiritual intelligence. To do this, management needs to treat people as "whole persons". The whole person consists of the body—for physical intelligence, the heart; for emotional intelligence, the mind; and for intellectual intelligence and spiritual intelligence, the soul.

The healthcare challenges most organisations face have to do with wellness, employee assistance programmes, sexual harassment, substance abuse, smoking, depression, HIV/AIDS, and conflict and violence at work.

The intersection between spiritual intelligence and a wellness programme will generate a holistic approach to healthcare and harmony in the workplace. Spiritual intelligence, in this context, means when people are living by their values/principles and conscience. It also implies having a clear sense of what is right and what is wrong. It instils in people the idea that they must have a meaning and purpose in life far beyond a career. Spiritual intelligence inspires people to live life fully by using all their talents and other resources. This topic has been covered extensively in my other book, *Become Extraordinary*. If people focus only on what is right in their personal and work life, they will harness inner peace and internal security.

The majority of people know that they need to have regular exercise in order to be fit and healthy. The body needs a certain level of aerobic respiration to burn any excess fat in the body. Similarly, the majority of people know that they need to eat a certain balanced diet in order to take care of their bodies. Excess fat in the body is a hazard and may lead to heart and/or blood disease. When people eat too many energy-dense foods, the body will just burn enough carbohydrates for the body processes and convert the rest to fat, which is stored in the body. Fat from fatty foods is also stored as fat in the body. This stored fat becomes a major threat to the body as it may cause or catalyse many diseases, especially those associated with the heart and blood circulation. A lot of people know that fruits and vegetables are healthy foods and that predominantly eating these kinds of foods will contribute a great deal to good health. Despite this knowledge, we still stuff our bodies with junk food. We let our appetites and not our conscience determine what we eat.

Following the whole-person paradigm, Stephen Covey indicates that spiritual intelligence affects the other human capacities such as the body, the mind, and the heart. "What happens to the body when spiritual intelligence is violated? People usually neglect their bodies; they often are burned out if they are not already worn out. Their minds are usually full of rationalization, which means telling oneself rational lies. They feel guilty, which is a healthy emotion when there is a genuine violation of integrity and conscience. They lack peace; they have impaired judgement. ... What happens to heart? These same people lose control over their emotions, their ability to understand others, to empathize with others. Their ability to have compassion and love for others is significantly diminished."

Regarding physical exercise, I have personally experienced that its benefits are not limited only to fitness and health. I have noticed that exercise also helps me to relieve stress and other emotional disorders. It also helps me relax my intellectual organs such as the brain. If I engage in physical exercise, it clears all the negative thoughts that I might have had prior to doing exercise. It has a spillover effect on my emotions, soul, and mind. On the physical front, exercise helps with strong muscles, giving the body energy, endurance, and flexibility. As can be seen, spiritually disciplining ourselves to have regular exercise can benefit our wellness in many areas.

Spirituality helps people to have the right frame of mind and an abundance of inner peace. Once people have the right frame of mind and abundant inner peace, they do not need employee assistance programmes. Spirituality in this sense is a preventative measure for social problems that would otherwise require assistance programmes. Social problems that may be caused by family, financial problems, and other personal pressures can have a very negative effect at work. Productivity can be affected drastically. Depression and other negative effects can increase, causing major damage to the individual's health at work.

Spirituality and the use of conscience can also help people to avoid such things as sexual harassment. This can contribute to a healthy and conducive work environment for people of different genders and different levels of seniority. Unnecessary conflicts are caused by sexual harassment, which itself is caused by the violation of a spiritual being. Sexual harassment can be prevented by respecting one's fellow workers and supporting equality.

Depression is one of the most common negative factors that eats up people who are deficient in spirituality. Depression may stem from divorce or a poor relationship with a loved one, financial problems, etc. People respond to depression in a number of ways. Some are able to share their problems with those close to them so they can receive friendly counselling. Some use illicit drugs to gain temporary relief from their problems. Some have learnt ways of dealing with negative feelings such as depression. Internationally Published author Anthony Robbins (in his book Awaken the Giant Within) cites that all human behaviour is adaptive in one way or another; it's designed to fill a need. Robbins came up with a six-step reframing process, as follows:

1) Identify the behaviour you want to change.
2) Establish communication with the part of your unconscious mind that generates the behaviour.
3) Separate intention from behaviour.
4) Create alternative behaviours to satisfy intention.
5) Have the part of the unconscious mind accept the new choices and the responsibility for generating them when needed.
6) Make an ecological check.

Some people have used the foregoing ideas or other techniques suggested by various professionals to cultivate spirituality with positive results. It is sometimes not so easy to practise these techniques to reap the benefits of positive spirituality.

Emotional Intelligence guru and international author Daniel Goleman cites that while depression can drive someone to drink, the metabolic effect of alcohol often simply worsens the depression after a short lift. More than half the patients being treated at a clinic for cocaine would have been diagnosed with severe depression before they started their habit. Spiritual intelligence is a powerful force in these situations as it helps people to reflect on and analyse their lives before they engage in behaviours that may lead to depression. Spiritual intelligence rightly guides individuals against the quick fixes to problems that have negative side effects, such as smoking, alcohol use, and the taking of drugs.

The adverse socioeconomic effects of HIV/AIDS has brought a lot of spiritual insight to many people. People have begun to take responsibility for their sexual practices in a positive way. People now know that it is right to stick with one partner, always to have safe sex, to know their partner's HIV status, and so on. They know that the more they do to prevent HIV infection and know their HIV status, the more they will be able to live responsibly and be happy.

People can develop spirituality in a number of ways. People who follow Christianity or any of the major religions develop spirituality by aligning to those principles in whatever they think or do. Preaching and ordinary counselling are also common tools of developing spirituality. Inspirational reading can also help educate the conscience by teaching us better ways of dealing with situations. Coaching, mentorship, and talking to role models are also powerful ways of developing people's spiritual side. The positive effects of exercise can also contribute to developing spiritual strength.

There is no doubt that if all employees in the workplace were spiritually intelligent, it would bring about holistic results and a harmonious working environment. People would have good interpersonal relationships.

People would have good emotional and physical health. People would be innovative and focused and would form complementary teams supportive of each individual involved. People would see each other as spiritual beings. There would be no conflicts or hidden agendas. People would always be fair and open to each other. But unfortunately this requires having great leadership in place to determine a spirituality programme and ensure that these principles are practised.

Training and Development

Many companies and government departments place a very low priority on training and development. However, this is very counterproductive in the knowledge worker age. Companies and institutions need to be on top of their game as far as training and development is concerned. Training and development has a very huge bearing on institutional results. The more employees know, the more they can produce. The first step to take is to perform a training and development needs assessment. This refers to the process used to determine if training is necessary or not. This process will highlight some training needs or pressure points and will bring forth some reasons why training is required. Some of these reasons or pressure points might be as follows:

- legislation
- lack of basic skills
- poor performance
- new technology
- customer requests
- new products
- higher performance standards
- new jobs
- business growth or contraction
- global business expansion

Once the reasons have been brought forth, the organisation then needs to determine who needs training. The decision needs to be made in the best interests of the organisation instead of in the best interests in individuals. The training must be outcome-based. What are the outcomes that needs to be achieved?

Some examples follow:

- what trainees need to learn
- who will receive training
- the type of training
- the frequency of training
- a buy versus build training decision
- training versus other HR options such as selection or job design
- how training should be evaluated

CHAPTER 10

DEVELOP GOOD INTERPERSONAL SKILLS

Emotional Intelligence

Leaders high in emotional self-awareness are attuned to their inner signals and recognise how their feelings affect them, their job performance, and how they relate to others. They are attuned to their guiding values and can often intuit the best course of action, seeing the big picture in a complex situation. Emotionally self-aware leaders can be candid and authentic, able to speak openly about their emotions or with conviction about their guiding vision. These leaders confidently solicit feedback from their juniors for future self-development.

It is imperative that leaders have a high degree of emotional self-control. They need to discover ways of managing their most negative emotions in the workplace, like anger, sadness, depression, frustration, guilt, regret, and embarrassment. Leaders also need to learn to stay calm and level-headed in difficult times or during a crisis. There will be times that are most trying for the organisation, and leaders need to remain clear-headed and manage their negative emotions. These kinds of leaders also ensure that there is transparency in almost everything they do. They are adaptable and never lose their focus on achievement. They always take initiative and responsibility. They have a high sense of optimism and enthusiasm.

Leaders with emotional social awareness are able to notice the emotional well-being of their colleagues and act in ways that ensure effective interactions and relationships with other people in the work environment. These leaders regard empathy as one of the keys to relating with emotionally disturbed employees.

Leaders with self-motivation capabilities are able to motivate themselves and their team members even when the going is tough and other people tend to hide their heads in the sand.

Effective Communication

Being an excellent communicator is an important skill for employees at all organisational levels. Effective communication skills are paramount in any kind of business. You communicate with your boss, your employees, your colleagues, and your clients. This being the case, an important part of the onboarding process is to foster an environment of open communication in your workplace, as well as to teach and nurture communication skills among new team members. But to succeed as a leader in today's frenetic business environment, you need to be able to capture and keep people's attention. Whether you are speaking informally with your team, presenting to a group of your colleagues, writing an email or report, or leading a meeting, your ideas are constantly competing for your listeners' or readers' focus. One moment they're following your analysis of third-quarter financials, and the next they're thinking about an email they have to respond to or their child's head cold. When we are on the receiving end of communication, we crave compelling, concrete, simple doses of information with an authentic voice. Creating this kind of communication requires careful planning and preparation, whether for writing or speaking, or in a memo, presentation, or meeting. For leaders, it is an essential skill. Leaders must communicate constantly in person, via telephone, in writing, and through electronic media.

John Mattone asserts that "leaders must also communicate effectively with a variety of people: employees at all levels, customers, vendors, suppliers, bosses, and, depending on their role, representatives of regulatory agencies, etc." The following is taken from Mattone (Talent Leadership)

- **Creating genuine relationships.** Being warm, open, and approachable; treating others with respect; and being regarded as a person of integrity
- **Communicating clearly.** Communicating accurate information in a clear and timely way, using constructive formal and informal channels to do so.
- **Listening fully.** Giving your full attention to others when they are communicating and accurately processing what is said with a minimum of personal bias.
- **Giving effective feedback.** Providing honest, clear, and respectful feedback to others in the organisation, and voluntarily soliciting feedback yourself and being open to what is said.
- **Managing conflict constructively.** Responding to conflict, both when you are directly involved and when you are not, with a problem-solving, nonblaming approach that produces successful outcomes.
- **Influencing others.** Being able to effectively and constructively influence others in a nonmanipulative way.

Five components of effective communication:

- sender
- receiver
- message
- medium
- feedback

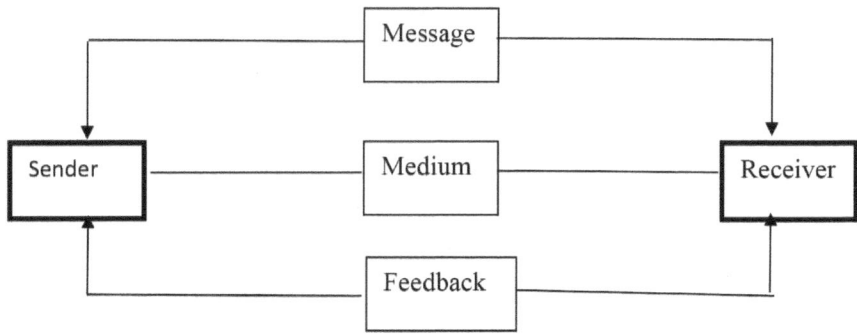

If you have matter to communicate, first ensure what is it that you want to communicate the (message). Then choose the right medium to use to communicate (that is verbal communication, email, memo, or some other method). Then observe the kind of feedback you receive to check how the communication is going. It must be the sender's intention for the message to be received at the other end. It is the sender's duty to send the right message and to be heard.

When we communicate, we convey the message using the three main components of communication. These components send the message in various ways.

Note how you communicate in terms of what people concentrate on while you are communicating:

- ❖ Body language   55 per cent
- ❖ Tone/voice projection 38 per cent
- ❖ Content   7 per cent

➢ Steps of Communicating/Questioning:

- ❖ Listen—Ensure you have the correct and relevant message.
- ❖ Internalise—Make sure you understand what you have heard.

- ❖ Paraphrase—Verify your understanding. (Repeat, ask questions.)
- ❖ Confirm—Confirm your understanding.
- ❖ Commit—Get commitment for action.

Effective Listening

In today's high-tech, high-speed, high-stress, information overload world, communication is more important than ever. A good part of effective communication is listening, yet we seem to devote less and less time to really listening to one another. Genuine listening has become a rare gift—the gift of time. I often hear people say that someone talks a lot, but I have never heard anybody say that someone listens a lot. This shows that listening is a rare commodity. Effective listening helps build relationships, solve problems, ensure understanding, resolve conflicts, and improve accuracy. At work, effective listening means fewer errors and less wasted time. At home, it stimulates love, trust, and respect, and it helps develop resourceful, self-reliant kids who can solve their own problems. Listening builds friendships and careers. It saves money and marriages.

I have come up with six steps to guide you in developing effective listening skills:

Step 1: Be attentive and maintain eye contact.

Good speakers are aware that communication needs attention from both the speaker and the listener. This demonstrates connection. It demonstrates that you are attentive to what is being said. If your attention drifts away to somewhere else, it will be viewed as distraction or lack of concentration. It is important to demonstrate that your mind is not wandering or gazing around. You need to be present to the conversation and appear to be paying attention to what is being said. You should not appear stressed or intimidating. Do not try to be efficient in your listening. Listening requires patience. If you are a fast thinker, slow your pace to accommodate the speaker. Be flexible and patient.

Step 2: Keep a clear and open mind.

Try to clear your mind of all other thoughts or opinions that are outside what is being communicated. Do not make judgements or criticisms. Do not make any conclusions before the communication has ended. Listen to the words and observe the feelings communicated nonverbally. Do not take over somebody's conversation in order to share your own experience. Do not interrupt or finish people's sentences. It might show impatience. Just respect that you are independent from the speaker and so his or her experiences will be different from yours.

Step 3: Create rapport with the speaker.

Listen to the words and observe the nonverbal signs. Remember that more than 90 per cent of communication is nonverbal. Observe the predominant words, predicates, submodalities, eye cues, facial expressions, and body gestures, and try to mirror these when possible. Try to follow the speaker's perception and not your own.

Step 4: Ask questions and confirm.

Ask questions that are relevant to the conversation when the speaker has paused. Ask mainly to confirm and to understand. Again, try not to interrupt when the speaker is in the middle of a sentence. If somehow you get the speaker off the topic, take responsibility and apologise, and then get the speaker back into the topic. Watch your questions to ensure their relevance as they will be good indicators as to whether you are concentrating on the conversation.

Step 5: Exercise empathy.

Notice the emotions of the speaker, and convey those feelings through your words and body language. If they feel sadness, express sadness and put yourself in their shoes. If they feel joyful, then express joy for them. If they feel fearful, convey fear to show you follow their fears. Empathy is a symptom of caring for other people. It really shows you are deeply listening and you care for emotional experiences people go through. When you express empathy, you have to show that you really understand what the other person is going through and that you are willing to assist if you can. Empathy makes people open up to you. It shows that you are generous and helpful, but more importantly that you care.

Step 6: Paraphrase and give feedback.

To demonstrate that you have been listening, you can paraphrase what the speaker has said. You can show that you understand what has been said by reflecting the emotions the speaker was exhibiting. If you cannot reflect the feelings, just paraphrase or summarise the speaker's content using the predominant words. Avoid indulging in your own fantasies. If the speaker has sought your opinion, give it only when you think you have fully understood the speaker.

As a way of improving your listening, do this exercise: For at least one week, at the end of every conversation in which information is exchanged, conclude with a summary statement. In conversations that result in agreements about future obligations or activities, summarising will not only ensure accurate follow-through but also will feel perfectly natural. In conversations that do not include agreements, if summarising feels awkward, just explain that you are doing it as an exercise.

Assertiveness, Aggressiveness, and Passiveness

Assertiveness has become a familiar but much misunderstood word in the modern world. This is ironic because assertiveness involves the ability to communicate clearly, specifically, and unambiguously, while at the same time being sensitive to the needs of others and their responses in a particular encounter. Assertiveness is based on a philosophy of personal responsibility and an awareness of the rights of other people. Being assertive simply means being honest with yourself and others. It means having the ability to say directly what you want, what you need, or what you feel, but not at the expense of other people.

Assertiveness is demonstrating respect for yourself and respect for another person. Assertiveness means having confidence in yourself and being positive, while at the same time understanding other people's points of view. It is being able to behave in a rational and adult way. Being assertive also means being able to negotiate and reach workable compromises. Above all, being assertive means having self-respect and respect for other people.

Assertiveness has three basic components:

- the ability to express feelings (for example, to accept and express anger, warmth, and sexual feelings);
- the ability to express beliefs and thoughts openly (being able to voice opinions, disagree, and take a definite stand, even if it is emotionally difficult to do so and even if you have something to lose in doing so); and
- the ability to stand up for personal rights (not allowing others to bother or take advantage of you). Assertive people are not shy; they are able to express their feelings and beliefs (often directly), and they do so without being aggressive or abusive.

Why Is Assertiveness Important?

There are two major reasons why it is important for people to learn how to be assertive in a way that allows them to say more directly what they really think, want, or feel without denying the thoughts, needs, or feelings of others.

The first and most obvious reason is that with this ability, people are much more likely to obtain more of what they want. Very often, this leads people to the subject of assertiveness in the first place, which in itself is a worthwhile goal. However, even with the ability to be assertive, people will not always be 100 per cent successful in obtaining all they want.

The second major reason for people to learn to be assertive is quite simply so they can feel good about themselves and their behaviour. This is just as important, although it may be initially less obvious. Difficult situations often arise unexpectedly, but some situations can be anticipated and planned for in order to communicate and act at some level and to some degree.

Being passive is a personality weakness. A passive person somewhat regards himself as inferior and as a victim. He lacks the guts to timeously stand up for his interests and wishes. He has a weakness in speaking for himself to preserve his wishes. He caves in and backs down easily and would have somebody else benefit at his own expense. But deep down, the passive person constantly feels unhappy and defeated because he compromises their interests.

There is also a challenge with passive-aggressive behaviour. It is like pressurising a bottle with carbon dioxide until it spontaneously explodes. People with this kind of behaviour will allow themselves to be pushed over, and over time they internally get wound up and plan revenge. Over time the bottled-up unhappiness suddenly explodes in their planned revenge and often with exaggeration and blowing things out of proportion. Their behaviour at this point is influenced by their emotions.

Aggression is another communication-related behaviour that some people adopt. It is normally influenced by anger or an inferiority complex. Aggressive people try to bulldoze other people with aggression to try to get what they want. Even though people with this kind of behaviour may experience short-term wins, their aggression-based behaviour never lasts for long. It is not sustainable in the long term. An aggressive person will inflict unnecessary stress upon herself, and other people will disrespect her and refuse to provide her with recognition. Then she will go into overdrive to counter that lack of respect or recognition.

Either way, there are two different things that we may carry forward from those occasions. The first is, what actually happened? The second is, how did I handle it?

In many difficult situations people often react by being aggressive, saying too much, too loudly, sometimes going way over the top, and then regretting it later. Alternatively, they may become passive, silent, holding back, saying and doing nothing and afterwards, thinking, *What should I have done?* or *What could I have said?* and feeling bad about themselves. In both circumstances this poor handling of the situation usually reinforces people's negative view of themselves and leads to a lack of self-respect.

Being assertive gives you inner peace with yourself and causes you to live in peace with the people around you. It allows you to state your thoughts and feelings with candour and conviction. There is normally no need for insistence or apology.

Being assertive is not:

- about getting your own way and winning every time
- a series of quick fix tricks or techniques to learn parrot fashion and then trot out in difficult situations
- a way of manipulating and managing other people so that you get your own way while looking as though you are considering others.

Who Is Assertiveness For?

The short answer to this is that assertiveness is for everyone. It is not remedial training for disadvantaged groups or individuals. It is developmental training that enables people at all ages and career stages to be more confident and able to say the right thing at the right time and in the right way with a much higher possibility of achieving the right outcome. Many organisations today integrate working with assertiveness into their mainstream management development programmes, along with problem-solving and staff supervision.

Core Skills and Beliefs

To become assertive, you need to address two areas; the first is about your views and beliefs. Do you believe you have the right to be assertive? Do you really see assertiveness as positive? What messages do you receive regarding assertive people? In order to believe you have the right to be assertive, you may need to work on unlearning some of the messages you have learned about yourself and your rights.

The second area of development relates to the skills of assertiveness. They are as follows:

- active listening
- body language
- broken record technique
- saying no
- creating a workable compromise
- fogging
- asserting negative feelings

Each of these skills may be practised and performed, but unless you really believe you have the right to be assertive, it is unlikely that you will put these skills into practice.

Assertiveness Is Not Aggression

A very common mistake is to confuse assertive behaviour with aggressive conduct. Indeed, this is why some people shy away from the very idea of assertiveness. To them it equals aggression; they fear that they'll hurt others or that they won't seem likeable. Not so—assertiveness is characterised by a clear statement of one's beliefs and/or feelings, accompanied by a consideration of the thoughts and feelings of others.

Let us now look at different types of communication as highlighted by the ICTO training institute:

The Aggressive Type

The aggressive type is marked by the following attitudes and behaviours:

- cannot afford to consider another person's point of view
- often has little self-esteem, so seeks self-aggrandisement through belittling others
- reacts in threatening situations by attacking outright
- is competitive and needs to prove his or her superiority by putting people down
- compulsively overreacts and often leaves, in his or her own wake, a trail of hurt and humiliated feelings
- leaves people around him or her feeling instantly defensive and, although they may not say so directly, harbouring resentful feelings towards him or her

The Passive Type

The passive type is marked by the following attitudes and behaviours:

- makes ideal fodder for the aggressive type
- sees himself or herself as a victim of unfairness and injustice at the hands of others
- finds it difficult to make decisions and allows others to decide for him or her (others will often resent this)
- clings to his or her hard-luck stories, resulting in the people around him or her feeling infuriated by his or her passivity and resignation
- often makes others feel initially guilty for not being able to do more to help, and after a while causes others to feel frustrated by his or her negative outlook and lack of willpower

- continually puts himself or herself down
- gives in or runs when faced with any kind of confrontation
- creates annoyance and irritation in others

The Manipulative Type

The manipulative type is marked by the following attitudes and behaviours:

- is skilled at deceiving himself or herself and others (this often stems from central low self-esteem)
- needs to control and manipulate those around in order to avoid getting hurt
- is never direct in his or her approach (this would be too risky)
- manages to satisfy most needs by subtly making others feel guilty if they don't do what he or she wants
- may appear to think highly of people close to him or her but often detect an undercurrent of disapproval, so they feel confused and often frustrated
- attacks, but—unlike the aggressive type—in a concealed manner, which makes it even more difficult for others to pin him or her down

The Assertive Type

The assertive type is marked by the following attitudes and behaviours:

- respects the people he or she is dealing with
- accepts his or her own positive and negative qualities and is able to be genuine in accepting other people
- does not need to put others down to feel OK
- feels OK with himself or herself
- doesn't believe that others are responsible for what happens to him or her, and takes responsibility for his or her own actions, decisions, and life

> doesn't have to make others feel guilty for not recognising his or her needs; can acknowledge his or her own needs and ask openly and directly, even though this risks refusal
> doesn't feel totally demolished when refused, because his or her self-esteem is anchored deeply within—it is not dependent on the approval of others
> is able to respond authentically to others' demands on his or her time and resources

Care

The Oxford Dictionary defines *care* as "a provision of welfare and protection and serious avoidance of damage, risk, or error". It goes on to indicate that care involves "feeling concern or interest for someone; feeling affection or liking—to look after and provide needs of".[6] When you treat people as human beings, you tend to care for them. When your ego is not obstructing you, you wilfully and genuinely show care for people. They then feel safe around you. Because they feel safe, they slowly begin to take down the protective armour they put on each morning before they leave home. They dismantle the barricade they have erected against the disappointment and discouragement they expect from the people in their lives. The person begins to see that you really care about them. The person begins to get that you want them to win. The person begins to realise that you have their best interests in mind. And so they begin to give you their very best.

Empathy

Empathy is the ability to recognise other people's emotions, to appreciate what they go through, and to put yourself in their shoes. It is being sensitive to why people behave the way they do. Empathy is a symbol of showing care for, interest in, and concern for other people. Many

---

6   "Care", Oxford Dictionaries, https://www.lexico.com/en/definition/care, accessed 24 Aug. 2019.

times empathy is confused with sympathy. Sympathy is when you feel for someone else's misfortune, whereas empathy is when you recognise and understand someone's feelings and you can place yourself in their situation. Empathy is also about seeing the world through another person's lens. Leaders have to develop empathy so that they can sense the emotional signals and dynamics of their team members. This allows them to show the necessary care and concern for their team.

Helpfulness

One of the most important aspects of leadership is to be helpful to others. It is knowing that it is your role to serve others and not to be served. This is the essence of moral authority as we have indicated earlier. The essence of every business is simply about being radically helpful. Always endeavour to do more than you are paid for. Your compensation will always be a direct function of your contribution. Affect many people's lives within your leadership circle. Be the change you want to see. Help other people to also make a difference.

Trust

What is trust to you? How do you build trust with your friends, family, and colleagues? Is it about doing what you said you are going to do and building relationships on honesty and integrity? How do you build trust in your relationships? As Ralph Waldo Emerson stated, "The glory of friendship is not an outstretched hand, not the kindly smile, nor the joy of companionship; it is the spiritual inspiration that comes to one when you discover that someone else believes in you and is willing to trust you with friendship."

One of your first tasks as a manager and leader is to gain the trust of your team. But your employees won't grant that trust automatically. As a leader, you have a profound effect on how they do their jobs and live their professional lives. As you take charge, they will have questions such as these: Will you be able to represent their work well to people outside the unit? Is it safe to speak up when they disagree with you? How will you act when faced with a difficult decision? Will you be an ally and an advocate?

Gaining trust can be a particularly delicate task when you have been promoted to manage your former peers. You need to establish authority and credibility without alienating those who used to have the same title as you—or who may even have been vying for the same job—and whose allegiance you now need.

Transparency

Transparency is all about being authentically open to others about what is going in the organisation. The openness must also account for people's feelings, beliefs, actions, and integrity. Leaders with integrity notice when they make mistakes, and they easily apologise. They do not hide their mistakes and faults. They also readily confront unethical behaviours they observe in others timeously rather than turn a blind eye to it.

Morale

Employee morale is the happiness, satisfaction, confidence, and overall positive outlook and attitude that employees feel and show at work. Employees with high morale are always excited to wake up early in the morning to go to work to excel and perform. They are quite open to meeting their most important career goals. High morale can only be achieved leaders who dedicate a lot of their time to people matters. If you spend the bulk of your time on the intangibles like morale and motivation, then the intangibles like results and sales will take care of themselves.

Motivation

Motivation is something special that points to the desires, needs, wants, and drive of the individual in the workplace. It is the psychological state of mind that drives or stimulates people to action to accomplish or achieve goals. From a leadership point of view, you need to be certain of those things likely to change people's behaviour so they'll want to achieve. Included could be the potential for promotion, success, self-fulfilment, job satisfaction, recognition, acceptance, and/or monetary rewards. These incentives will vary from organisation to organisation. It is the leader's utmost responsibility to search for the things that make people tick and give them the willingness to perform at their best capabilities.

Inspiration

Leaders need to breathe life, energy, passion, and excitement into people through their compelling vision and purpose. Such leaders model the behaviours they ask of others. They walk the talk. They are able to effectively communicate the organisation's and their own vision so it becomes a shared vision that inspires everyone else. They are able to translate the shared vision into everyone's day-to-day tasks.

Organisational Awareness

Leaders need to have the social awareness to read those organisational forces that determine how people relate in the organisation and how they form social networks. Leaders need to establish the political dynamics that influence the behaviour of individuals in the organisation. Leaders also need to notice the prevailing culture of the institution. The culture spells out the guiding values and unspoken rules in the organisation that make people believe that "this is how we do things here".

Service

Leaders need to be just as focused on customer service as much as front-line employees are. Leaders must serve the customers through serving the front-line employees. If you want your customers to be treated well, then treat your front-line employees well. In fact, treat all your employees well.

Developing Others

Great leaders focus on nourishing human capital. They look for potential and develop it. They look for positive attitude for development and water it. These leaders are able to balance employee aspirations and organisational needs. The tools include but not are limited to training, empowerment, delegation, mentoring, and coaching. People's career goals, work performance, performance feedback, work attitude, strengths, and weaknesses will be a guideline on which tools to use.

Change Catalyst

Leaders see the need for the creation and mobilisation of change. Great leaders are uncomfortable with the status quo. They understand that change is inevitable, so they know there is a need to change the process of how they do things and look for better ways. They are people who make things happen not only to meet expectations but also to exceed them. They also find ways to manage resistance to change.

Conflict Management

There will always be conflicts in the workplace. Because of this, one of the most powerful responsibilities a leader has is to effectively manage conflicts. Leaders need to give themselves the opportunity to understand the differing perspectives and help all parties find a common solution.

Teamwork and Collaboration

A leader needs to be player number one in his or her team. Experts in teamwork have demonstrated that a team is only as strong or effective as its leader is. A leader must model all ingredients of effective teamwork such as respect, helpfulness, cooperation, communication, unity, and togetherness. The leader needs to know the competence of each team member and use it towards the best of the team. The leader gets the team focused on common goal and gets the absolute commitment of each member to achieve that common goal. It is the leader's role to build a unique team spirit and identity that gives each member something to be proud of.

Influence

Leaders need to enact or influence people's beliefs and actions. Leaders need to get buy-in into what they seek to achieve. A leader needs to create a momentum of performance among the people he or she leads. Leaders need to be able to persuade people so they become willing to be engaged and perform.

CHAPTER 11
DRIVE FOR RESULTS

Organisations exist for specific purposes. Associated with those purposes are results. An organisation exists to produce results. For an organisation to be well-positioned to produce results, it needs to come up with or craft a great strategy and an organisational statement expressing what it is about—and then go on to execute that strategy. A. A. Thompson Jr. et al. published a powerful book called *Crafting and Executing Strategy*. From this I have distilled eight steps that can be taken to position your organisation to deliver great results:

1. Setting the Overall Direction or Strategic Vision

Top management needs to come up with the overall direction the organisation needs to take. This vision can be made early on in the organisation's life or during the periodic strategy-making or review process. A well-crafted vision should not change frequently. The strategic vision expresses clearly the aspirations top management have for the organisation. It also gives a bird's-eye view of where the organisation is going and a convincing rationale of why it makes business sense for the organisation to go in that direction.

2. Communicating the Strategic Vision

Effectively communicating the strategic vision to lower managers and front-line employees is as important as coming up with the well-formed strategic vision itself. Not only do people have a need to believe that senior management know where they're trying to take the organisation and understand what changes lies ahead both externally and internally, but also, unless and until front-line employees understand why the strategic course that management has charted is reasonable and beneficial, lower-tier employees are unlikely to rally behind managerial efforts to get the organisation moving in the intended direction. Communicating the strategic vision to employees must include a clear picture of where the organisation is going and why it is going in that direction. Members of the executive team must be tasked with the role of communicating the vision to every employee as is feasibly possible.

3. Setting Strategic Objectives

Setting objectives is the process of converting the strategic vision into specific performance targets—results and outcomes that the organisation wants to achieve. Objectives represent a managerial commitment to achieving particular results and outcomes. Well-stated objectives are quantifiable or measurable and contain a deadline for achievement. As Bill Hewlett, cofounder of Hewlett-Packard, observes, "You cannot manage what you cannot measure. … And what gets measured gets done." Setting concrete and measurable objectives creates a yardstick used to measure the organisation's performance and progress. I have observed that to be able to track performance well, the strategic objectives need to be turned into a balanced scorecard format that can be tracked on a regular basis. The objectives can be reviewed annually for opportunities to stretch them for even better performance.

4. Crafting the Strategy

A. A. Thompson Jr. et al. assert that the task of crafting the strategy entails answering a series of how questions: how to grow the business, how to please customers, how to outcompete rivals, how to respond to changing market conditions, how to manage each functional piece of the business and develop needed competencies and capabilities, and how to achieve strategic and financial objectives. It also means exercising astute entrepreneurship in choosing from among the various strategic alternatives and proactively searching for opportunities to do new things or to do existing things in new or better ways. The key question here is who gets involved in the strategy formulation. My take is that it will be the senior leadership, unit heads, and other key managers and stakeholders who will have special or unique role to play in the strategy formulation. If there are specialists who are likely to be involved or affected by the strategy, they must not be excluded from the formulation team. The strategy formulation will then involve conducting a SWOT (Strengths, Weaknesses, Opportunities and Threats) analysis of the organisation and translating it into strategic actions.

5. Implementing and Executing the Strategy

This is the step where everything starts happening. The strategic plans that have been developed are now converted into action and results. This is where the managers get to come up with activities and actions in their section or unit to execute their piece of the strategic plan. This is where the organisation will be able to manage organisational change, build and strengthen organisational competencies, motivate people, create and nurture a strategic and supportive work climate, and meet or beat performance targets. Normally after the strategy development, the organisation needs to restructure itself to ensure that it has the right skills and expertise to execute and implement the strategy. Some jobs may be reviewed to ensure they better fit the requirements of strategy execution. The organisation leadership need to source and avail the necessary resources required for strategic success. The leadership need to ascertain that the current policies and procedures will also support strategic implementation. Benchmarking activities can also be employed to ensure that best practices are used. Organisational culture, employee behaviour, and work climate are modified to suit the successful strategy execution. Motivation, rewards, and incentives are also reviewed to ensure they are directly relevant to the achievement of performance objectives aligned with the strategy.

6. Evaluating Performance and Initiating Correcting Adjustments

This is the evaluation and monitoring stage of the strategy management process. At this stage, the company evaluates how it is doing in relation to the implementation of the strategy. The organisation will monitor internal progress and external developments. The leadership need to assess whether performance targets are met to their satisfaction. They will also have to assess whether the external factors that triggered the strategy, such as industry and competitive conditions, are in line with the organisation's success. If everything looks favourable, leadership will decide to stay on course with the strategy. If things look bad, again leadership need to decide whether it is the result of poor strategy, poor strategy execution, or both. Leadership then need to take appropriate corrective action.

The organisation may have to go back to the drawing board and review the entire process again, that is the strategic vision, the objectives, and the strategy itself. It might also be possible that some aspects of the strategy implementation process were not done well. In all the factors outlined herein, if an anomaly is noticed, then corrective adjustments need to be made.

In producing results, leaders need to lead the way. They must model the way. They must be models of the behaviours they expect of others. Exemplary leaders go first. They go first by setting the example through their actions that demonstrate they are deeply committed to their beliefs.

Every organisation exists for the achievement of results. The results can be in the form of products, services, purpose/mission, economy, or development. The success of a business organisation is measured by the business' profitability. The success of a nonprofit organisation is measured by how well it achieves its purpose. The success of a country is measured by how well it grows its economy, how well it develops, and the level of happiness of its people. From the country point of view, I always get inspired by the American dream that steered the

United States to become the most powerful country in the world. It was through exceptional leadership that the country became successful.

The American dream states that the ideal that government should protect each person's opportunity to pursue his or her own idea of happiness.

The Declaration of Independence protects this American dream. It uses the familiar quote: "We hold these truths to be self-evident, that all men are created equal, that they are endowed by their Creator with certain unalienable Rights that among these are Life, Liberty and the pursuit of Happiness."

The Declaration continues, "That to secure these rights, Governments are instituted among Men, deriving their just powers from the consent of the governed." The Founding Fathers put into law the revolutionary idea that each person's desire to pursue happiness was not just self-indulgence. It was a part of what drives ambition and creativity. By legally protecting these values, the Founding Fathers set up a society that was very attractive for those aspiring to a better life.

As an entrepreneur, I know what business success is. When the products and services are acquired, you know that there is business success. When the products and services do not get acquired, you know that there is no success.

When leaders are not focused on results, they are acting very irresponsible for their organisations. I have run a number of other organisations in my career, including a copper and nickel mining business production department, a diamond mining business production department, a nonprofit organisation, a local, national, and international unit, a Roman Catholic church parish, and a local community football club. With all of these, I can tell you that the results were at the top of my agenda and the priority of my focus. If I did not get the results I sought, I knew that there was a challenge with my leadership or with my team.

If the challenge was with leadership, I always tried to improve my leadership. If the problem was with my team, I always tried to improve my leadership team.

The production of results is where leadership really takes off and shifts into another gear. The production of results is what qualifies and separates true leaders from people who merely occupy leadership positions. Good leaders always make things happen. They get results. They can make a significant impact on an organisation.

Let us pause to determine what the results for your organisation and for you as the leader are. First let us look at organisations. A business organisation's results is determined by how much profit it makes. The results of a nonprofit or nongovernmental organisation are measured by how well the organisations fulfils its mission. The results of a government are determined by how well it implements its policies to ensure a conducive environment for business to thrive, ensure economic growth, and ensure adequate health and education, development of infrastructure, and empowerment of its people. Leaders who produce results not only are productive individually but also are able to help the team produce. This ability gives productive leaders confidence, credibility, and increased influence. No one can fake production. Either you're producing for the organisation and adding value to the bottom line or you're not.

Many of the people who will read *Extraordinary Leadership* are going to be leaders, managers, and supervisors. For supervisors, the role I expect them to play is to supervise work and the worker at the front line of the organisation. For managers, the role I expect them to play is to control and maintain systems, processes, procedures, resources, plans, and budgets. For leaders, the role I expect them to play is to influence the organisation and to lead on the intangible items such as vision, inspiration, motivation, morale, accountability, energy, timing, and culture. Extraordinary leaders ensure they have a high level of self-discipline, a strong work ethic, and the skills to remain productive.

Organisations need employees who can deliver results on a consistent basis. Organisations need leaders who are results-oriented and who move their employees to deliver results on a consistent basis. Let's take a look at a quote from Peter Drucker: "There are two types of people in the business community: those who produce results and those who give you reasons why they didn't."

Success, and more specifically results, is a product of productivity. Leaders need to know what makes their employees productive and must keep them productive. Productive leaders produce the results themselves. They walk the talk and lead by example. Productive leaders put people at the head of the class. Anyone who can produce has a chance to influence others. Productive leaders serve as an example to the people they lead, and their productivity sets the standard for the team. Productive leaders communicate the vision through action. When followers see positive results and see goals being met, they get a clearer picture of what it means to fulfil the vision. Productive leaders help their people to see what productivity looks like. And with each day of productivity, the team gets one step closer to making the vision a reality. That encourages members of the team. It validates their efforts. It makes the vision clearer.

Leaders cannot delegate problem-solving to someone else. They have to be active in breaking through obstacles, putting out fires, correcting mistakes, and directing people. Thomas Carlyle observes, "Nothing builds self-esteem and self-confidence like accomplishment." Productivity is inspiring. People who feel good about themselves often produce good results. And good results create positive momentum and high morale. High morale stimulates production. Productivity creates morale. Leaders who can produce positive results always have a positive impact on their team. Morale is a state of mind. It involves steadfastness, courage, and hope. It is confidence, zeal, and loyalty. When well-led organisations sustain high morale and high productivity over a long period, they gain momentum, which is any leader's best friend. Momentum helps a leader do anything and everything more easily. Without momentum, everything is harder to do than it should be. With it, everything is easier.

Who wants to leave a championship team? No one. People simply love being on a winning team. Winners attract people. The key to building a winning team is recognising, selecting, and retaining the best of the people you attract.

Colin Powell asserted, "You can issue all the memos and give all the motivational speeches you want, but if the rest of the people in your organization don't see you putting your best effort every single day, they won't either." (Source: Maxwell, 2011)

Producers and achievers always have an impact on the people who work with them and for them. Productive leaders are an example to the people they lead, and their productivity sets the standard for the team. When leaders produce, so do their people. Productive leaders thrive on results—from themselves and the team. They show the way, and others follow.

Good leaders constantly communicate the vision of the organisation. They do it clearly, creatively, and continually. But that doesn't mean that everyone who gets the message understands and embraces it. The production level of leadership communicates the vision through action, which helps people to understand in ways they may not have before. When followers see positive results and see goals being met, they get a clearer picture of what it means to fulfil the vision.

Leaders have to be active in solving problems, breaking through obstacles, putting out fires, correcting mistakes, and directing people.

Adaptability

Modern businesses operate in a quickly changing world. Change is the new normal. Therefore leaders need to be flexible and adaptable to the change that comes their way. If leaders are not flexible, their organisations will be eaten alive by the competitors who are able to deal with the change. Organisations face internal and external challenges, and they need to be agile.

Achievement

As has been indicated earlier, leaders must have an achievement drive—both for themselves and for the people they lead. They must seek consistent performance. They also look for opportunities to improve. They challenge the status quo and seek better ways of achievement. They must also reasonably stretch themselves and others.

Initiative

Leaders lead by example in taking initiative. They are always proactive and take responsibility for results. They plan what they are going to do, and then they carry out those plans. They manage themselves to guard against procrastination. They are always looking for opportunities, and when opportunities come, they seize them. Leaders also innovate and seek innovation from others. They timeously remove obstacles such as obsolete procedures and red tape.

Optimism

Leaders who are optimistic always see the glass as half full as opposed to half empty. They always have a positive outlook of the future even when failure seems imminent. They turn obstacles into opportunities. They look for ways to turn adversities into victories.

CHAPTER 12
EFFECTIVE PERFORMANCE MANAGEMENT

Performance management is used to ensure that the employees' activities and outcomes are congruent with the organisation's objectives. It entails specifying those activities and outcomes that will result in the firm's successfully implementing the strategy. For example, companies that are "steady state" (not diversified) tend to have evaluation systems that call for subjective performance assessments of managers. This stems from the fact that those above the first-level managers in the hierarchy have extensive knowledge of how the work should be performed. On the other hand, diversified companies are more likely to use quantitative measures of performance to evaluate managers because top-level managers have less knowledge about how work should be performed by those below them in the hierarchy.

Similarly, executives who have extensive knowledge of the behaviours that lead to effective performance use performance management systems that focus on the behaviours of their subordinate managers. However, when executives are unclear about the specific behaviours that lead to effective performance, they tend to focus on evaluating the objective performance results of their subordinate managers (Noe et al.).

The best performance measurement system known is the 360-degree performance feedback or appraisal system. It is indicated that the

360-degree performance appraisal system was first used in the 1940s. This method of appraisal is compared to having multiple points on a compass by dividing the circle into four equal dimensions of 90 degrees each. It provides the opportunity for an employee to receive a holistic assessment and feedback according to four main dimensions in the workplace. The employee is appraised by and receives feedback from self, subordinates, peers/customers, and ultimately the supervisor. The company that popularised the 360-degree appraisal system is General Electric (GE), which they did in the 1990s. The nature of the 360-degree appraisal system is that it collects performance and competency assessment information from multiple sources who observe and are affected by the performance of the employee.

The 360-degree appraisal system is ideally used to assess performance and competency at the supervisory, middle management, and senior management level. It can also be used for positions that render special or professional service in the institution, whether technical or otherwise. The complexity of these roles enables organisations to get holistic assessments from various people who have a stake in the organisation's business. It also offers the opportunity to generate objective assessments of the organisation's human resources.

The world's smartest organisations use 360-degree assessments in both performance and competence to enhance the organisation's HRM decisions on matters such as remuneration, promotions, talent management, and training and development. Some organisations may calibrate the raw assessment results to fit a bell curve for remuneration purposes. But those raw assessments remain important for other HRM decision-making purposes given their objective nature. The 360-degree assessment is comprehensive and objective because the feedback comes from all sources in the four-dimensional 360-degree scenario.

Advantages of 360-degree appraisal:

- Offers a more comprehensive view of the performance of employees.
- Improves credibility of the performance appraisal.
- Colleague feedback helps strengthen self-development.
- Increases the sense of responsibility of employees to their customers.
- The mix of ideas can give a more accurate assessment.
- Opinions gathered from many varied staff are sure to be more persuasive.
- Not only does the manager assess staff performance, but also other colleagues do.
- People who undervalue themselves are often motivated by feedback from others.
- If more staff take part in the process of performance appraisal, the organisational culture of the company becomes more honest.

Disadvantages of 360-degree appraisal:

- Takes a lot of time and is complex in administration.
- Exchange of feedback can cause trouble and tensions among staff.
- Training is required and important, as is putting forth effort in order to achieve efficiency in work.
- It is very hard to figure out the results.
- Feedback can be useless if it is not carefully and smoothly dealt with.
- It can impose an environment of suspicion if the information is not openly and honestly managed.

Who should conduct the 360-degree performance appraisal?

Whatever approach to performance management is used, it is necessary to decide whom to use as the source of the performance measures. Each source has specific strengths and weaknesses. We will discuss five primary sources:

- self
- subordinates
- peers/customers
- superior
- anyone who comes into contact with the employee and can provide valuable insights and information

It is worth noting that for the 360-degree appraisal to remain objective, the performance objectives must be accurately set at the beginning of the appraisal period. If the objectives are inaccurately or loosely set, then the process will not be objective. The old saying "garbage in, garbage out" kicks in.

Self

Self-assessment ratings may not necessarily be a good source of performance information for reasons of bias, but they are important if one seeks to know the employees' views of their performance. It is also important to have access to the information that the employees have about the results of their job and to observe their behaviour in as far as their performance is concerned. In as far as bias is concerned, there is a natural tendency for individuals to inflate their assessments in an effort to try to achieve high performance ratings. The cause of this bias is mainly that performance assessments are interlinked with other important factors such as pay increases, promotions and career progression, talent management, and training and development. The individual may also try to inflate ratings if he wants to blame other, external factors for his low ratings, for example his interfacing with coworkers. Despite all these drawbacks, self-performance appraisals are important to get all the employee's views about his performance and to set a baseline for the performance feedback discussions. It is important to compare the employee's comments about his performance with those of other stakeholders in the performance process. If the performance management is done regularly, for example monthly or quarterly, the bias alluded to can be minimised. The important thing about these self-ratings is to ensure they are based on the preset performance objectives and are in line with the balanced scorecard reviews.

Subordinates

Subordinates' performance assessments are an important source of information on performance. In supervisory, management, and leadership roles, it is expected that subordinates form part of their superior's performance team(s). Therefore they must know the key performance objectives of their superior (through the team's objectives) and his or her contribution to the performance against those objectives. Again the balanced scorecard review of information will be key in this review. The way this ideally works is to determine a few of your subordinates (say, three or five) and agree with your superior that they will be the ones involved in the performance appraisal. This agreement is important so as to eliminate subjectivity, which can occur when choosing a few subordinates who are friendly towards you and are likely to show you favour. The ratings of the subordinates, together with their comments for those ratings, are important for the rest of the performance appraisal process. These ratings give a view independent of the individual about her performance. The objectivity of this feedback depends on whether the evaluations are done on an anonymous basis. What this implies is that the manager must not know where each individual evaluation came, that is from which individual subordinate. This eliminates fears of retribution and intimidation from the managers being appraised. Subordinates are an especially valuable source of performance information when managers are evaluated.

Peers

Peers and/or colleagues at the same level as the employee are also an important source of performance information. These people are important in that the superior may not necessarily receive all the performance information. Assuming that these peers are team members of the superior's sectional or departmental team, they will know the preset performance objectives of the individual under review. They will have expert knowledge of the job requirements and performance targets and also will be likely to be in touch with the day-to-day activities of the individual being evaluated. Just like with subordinates, the ratings of the peers together with their comments about their ratings are important for the rest of the performance appraisal process. It also gives a view independent from the individual about his performance. If they have been preselected randomly, peers are expected to give a more professional performance appraisal in line with the individual's entire business performance. Even though peers may be viewed as competitors for upward progression of the individual under review, it is also expected that they take cognizance of their personal integrity in doing an objective appraisal of their coworker. Again, care must be taken to avoid appraisals done by potential personal friends in the workplace, which may render the performance ratings subjective.

Customers

One way or another, each individual in the workplace is providing service to one or more customers, whether internal or external. The performance feedback from these customers is very valuable to the performance review of the individual. It is normally expected that these customers know the performance objectives of the individual as they should be in line with customer expectations. Customers generally have no reason to show the individual unqualified favour. If the individual meets customer expectations, then she meets them—and if she doesn't, then she doesn't. That's it. Therefore, it is generally expected that the performance appraisal done by customers is objective.

Superior

Most organisations use supervisors, managers, and leaders as the only source of performance information. This stems from the assumption that these people have adequate knowledge of the job requirements of the individual being appraised, that they consistently observe the individual at work, and hence they can provide trustworthy performance assessments. But unfortunately, due to the fact that people lack leadership maturity and competence within these roles, the foregoing assumptions are baseless. There are so many things that cloud the objectiveness of performance assessments in there are no checks and balances. Managers are self-centred, insecure, and undeveloped, and have personal differences with subordinates, etc. They therefore use performance assessments as a tool to settle workplace scores. This then renders the performance assessments from managers subjective. There is also a lot of favouritism in the workplace, contributing to the subjectiveness of the performance ratings of some individuals.

To eliminate these potential inaccuracies, the 360-degree evaluation system is the solution to bias and favouritism. Assuming that the individual may be selfish in his self-ratings, the other evaluators, such as subordinates, peers, and customers, provide a good point of reference for objectivity since all ratings are measured against the very same objectives that were agreed at the beginning of the appraisal period.

Performance objectives must never be changed in the middle of the period unless an individual changes jobs in the middle of the appraisal period. Performance reviews are valuable to your organisation and therefore must be done delicately and in the best possible of ways. The information you collect and codify will help your organisation make valid decisions about remuneration, talent management, training and development, success planning, and promotions, along with a whole range of strategic decisions pertaining to the organisation. And when it comes to difficult employees, performance reviews must be done in such a way that both the employee and the organisation are protected. There could be lawsuits from employees who have been fired, demoted, or denied a merit increase because of a performance review.

A good performance management system is of strategic importance to all business, government, and NGO institutions. A good 360-degree evaluation system is normally well used in conjunction with the balanced scorecard. When they are used together, they eliminate all subjectivity from the performance process. Great business and government institutions have in place both of these systems. The 360-degree appraisal system is used both in performance management and in the competency assessment processes. Competency assessments are important in that they ensure that the right individuals are placed in the right jobs or positions. They also factor into other important aspects such as succession planning, promotions, and employee development. Performance assessments are important in ensuring that all human capital of the institution are effectively contributing to the success of the institution's business.

Upon placement in the job, each employee must be well conversant with what the job entails and how it contributes to the bigger picture of the business. The description of the job must also come down to the assessment metrics of measuring performance, which in most cases are called key performance indicators (KPIs). The KPIs of each employee must be consistent with the organisational strategy depending at where they are in the organisational chart. Each employee must also be clear on the frequency at which performance management will be conducted. There must be consistency within and compliance with this established frequency. All stakeholders must contribute to the success of the performance management system.

At the beginning of the appraisal period, each and every employee must agree to the performance measurements. These agreements must be designed in line with the job descriptions and the established KPIs. The performance measurements agreement must be signed by each employee and his or her immediate superior. Then these performance objectives must be communicated to all stakeholders in the performance management process.

The human resources department must ensure that the performance assessment of every employee be conducted at every performance management system calendar point established for the organisation.

Extraordinary Leadership

It is mandatory that every employee be given performance assessment feedback after each appraisal period. Any manager found not to have done performance assessments or given associated feedback without an acceptable reason must be subjected to disciplinary action. I know that most managers create little time for doing performance appraisals. This should be treated as a performance factor in itself. I also know that most managers do not like having to confront their subordinates in the process of giving performance assessment feedback. Again this must be treated as a performance factor for all supervisors and managers. However, great leaders make every manager accountable to ensuring the assessments are done. They ensure there is ongoing review, full employee involvement, and more importantly, recognition for high performance.

The following summarises the performance management procedure:

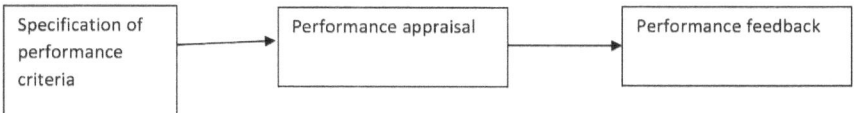

CHAPTER 13
EFFECTIVE DELEGATION

In my working with supervisors, managers, and leaders from various organisations, I have noticed that delegation was a major challenge to most of these roles. Delegation is, however, one of your most important responsibilities in these roles. To delegate well, you have to ensure that you get the right person to do the right job at the right time and in his or her own way. The work that you would delegate is the work that under normal circumstances would be done by you, but for some valid reason you have found the need to delegate.

Effective delegation will assist the manager in freeing up some valuable time to do strategic work such as planning work assignments, organising resources, planning employee development, doing performance management, addressing morale or climate issues, and coaching people. Delegation will not get you entirely free for doing this work, but the idea is to create time for the high-priority and high-impact work you must do for the organisation. Delegation should not be used as an excuse for incompetence or laziness. One of the reasons why a manager would delegate, as indicated above, would be to free up some time for strategic work. Another reason would to develop, empower, and grow his or her juniors. Delegation requires that a manager develop his or her subordinates and absolute trust that they are able to deliver. It might not mean that they can entirely do the work, but if they get stuck, they can come and ask for assistance.

Some managers struggle to delegate some of their work because they are weak in developing their people. These kinds of managers find themselves having to do the bulk of their work even when they are overwhelmed. Some do not delegate because of insecurity resulting from their own incompetence. For a manager to delegate, she must be competent herself, willing to develop her juniors, and have aspirations to move on herself. Bear in mind that in most institutions, you cannot be promoted if you have not developed your successors—even when you yourself are due for promotion. You have to incrementally develop your team members to the point where any delegated work would not be too much of a stretch for your team.

You have to be open with your team and not keep them from the opportunity of doing some of your work for you. But they must do well in their own work first before they can be delegated to. When you delegate, you still maintain accountability to deliver good results. Ensure you avail yourself of delegation when you need assistance, but ensure not to micromanage. Also ensure that you do not overburden only a few members of your team. When you delegate well, you benefit, your team members benefit, and your organisation benefits. You benefit in that you now have time to do other strategic tasks that you would otherwise not be able to get to, and you also have a chance to develop your team. Your team members get the opportunity to grow in their careers and their jobs. The organisation benefits in that it now has an increased pool of competent and well-developed employees. Delegation increases the spirit of teamwork, communication, and problem-solving, and it improves motivation in the team. Delegation should not be done haphazardly. It must be planned well.

Developing a Delegation Plan

Once you have identified a task to delegate, start by making a written delegation plan before you talk to your employee. It should detail everything from why the assignment is important to the deadlines involved.

The plan you make must be gear towards the long-term vision of the organisation and the aspirations of the employee. The delegation plan must consider the skills, competencies, and attitudes of the employee. If you delegate to someone who does have the skills and competencies, it might be a call for failure, disappointment on your side, and frustration on the side of the employee. If you delegate to someone who does not have a good employee, you might risk not getting quality work done. Delegation must also take cognizance of the employee's current job assignments so as not to create work overload and burnout for the employee.

A delegation plan must be part of the general employee development and empowerment strategy. All delegation plans must be transparent. The delegation plan must be written so it may be referred to at a later stage. It must carry with it all the necessary information an employee needs to know to take over the job being delegated. It must outline the necessary accountability, responsibility, and authority entailed. Effective delegation is one of those key ingredients that individuals must possess in order to succeed as a supervisor, as a committee chairperson, or in some other position in which they lead people. To effectively carry out your responsibilities as an organisation leader, it is important to delegate work. Delegating is more than simply handing out work or projects. To effectively delegate, remember these following steps:

Step 1: Make a delegation decision. Decide what to delegate.

Review the number of tasks, projects, and functions on your plate, and decide which ones you can comfortably delegate. Assess the skill levels of your direct reports to see if they match the complexity of the work. Confirm whether the delegation will require any guidance, coaching, or on-the-job training. Delegate those jobs that could be explained by articulating exactly what needs to be done. Do not make it look like you are delegating tasks because you are incompetent and cannot do them yourself or because you do not like doing them. Avoid delegating tasks that require specialised skills that only you have. If the work requires specialised skills, train your employees first to empower them with the necessary skills. If you are certain they have acquired the skills, then you can go ahead and delegate the work. Be clear on what responsibilities you will delegate along with the work.

Step 2: Determine the purpose of delegation.

Decide why you are delegating the work. Is it purely to minimise your own workload so you can focus on more strategic duties, or is it for empowerment purposes?

Step 3: Determine the content of the job to be delegated.

What exactly is the content of the job to be delegated? Put a definition on the job so that it can be clearly communicated, including the results to be achieved. Is the job something routine, like a monthly report, or it a one-off project? Is it a function like chairing a meeting? If it is a routine task, you may give a sample of a similar previous job for reference. If it is a new project, explain in detail the results and outcomes that the project is trying to achieve and the resources available for use. If it is a function, again give an explanation of the outcomes, and also give the guidelines for effective achievement. The level of explanation must suit the level of experience and skill of the person the job is delegated to.

Step 4: Decide who will be suitable to perform the work.

Decide who among your direct reports will be the right person to perform the task, project, or function. Make decisions based on the employee's skill level, experience, motivation, work attitude, current workload, availability, etc. In choosing the person, make it clear that you are not taking advantage of your direct reports. Communicate clearly the reason for delegation identified in step 2.

Step 5: Decide on and communicate the deadline for the assignment.

Decide on the deadline to give to your direct report. When should he deliver the final outcomes to you for assessment? Get commitment from the employee to confirm whether your deadline is reasonable. If the work is destined to go to your superior, ensure that the deadline given will give you enough time to review and fine-tune the work if there is need.

Step 6: Give guidelines on the process.

If it is the first time the person is doing this type of work, give him guidelines on the process to be followed. Do not give too much, though, because then it might look like lack of intellectual trust. Be clear on the amount of authority given to the employee in terms of making decisions. Be clear on the budget and other resources required for the work.

Step 7: Motivate the worker.

- When delegating a task or job, motivate the worker by explaining the importance of the task.
- Don't give the impression that you are delegating the task simply because no one else wants it or it is not important.

Step 8: Turn it over, assign responsibility, and grant authority.

- Once you delegate a task, let the team member complete it.
- Show trust (i.e. don't constantly check on the worker).
- It is important that the worker have the authority to complete the task and make decisions.

Step 9: Encourage independence, yet provide encouragement.

- Team members may need structure and guidance initially, but after a while, encourage them to work independently.
- Periodically touch base to see if they have any questions or problems.

Step 10: Give feedback and support.

Step 11: Maintain control.

Step 12: Remember that you are ultimately responsible for the work and its eventual success or failure.

CHAPTER 14
GIVING EFFECTIVE FEEDBACK

At the outset, I need to acknowledge the Harvard Business School. For this chapter, I used some of their ideas in the *Harvard Business Review Manager's Handbook*.

Giving your employees feedback is critical to helping them succeed in their jobs. There are various kinds of feedback that can be given to an employee in a work situation. Positive feedback may be given for a particular job well done, or corrective feedback may be given for a job not well done. There are also feedback sessions related to the performance management system and competency assessments. Positive feedback reinforces good work. Praise and coaching advice can create genuine bonds between you and your employees. Those moments when you tell your direct report, "You've done a great job! Congratulations," are powerful connections that build their trust and respect for you as a leader.

Corrective feedback urges the recipient to change course or adjust practices that aren't working. Managers, even experienced supervisors, often dread these conversations. Nobody likes having to tell a direct report that his work is below par or that he needs to adjust his attitude. But when handled well, these conversations produce real change in your value for employee behaviours, skills, and outcomes. These interactions create value for you (i.e. a more productive team), for your organisation (i.e. better outcomes), and for the employees (i.e. pride in their resilience and growth).

When you are preparing to give a performance review, when you are looking for ways to turbocharge a star's abilities, or when you simply need to help a struggling employee get back on track, this chapter will help you deliver feedback in a way that your employee can hear, understand, and implement.

When giving feedback, the manager needs to personally detach himself or herself from all personal differences or clashes with the employee so the feedback is effective. If there are some relationship or attitude issues with regard to a particular employee, seeking a third-party witness such as a human resources partner may be ideal to ensure the process moves smoothly or for potential mediation. Do not use feedback sessions as opportunities to get revenge, square up on differences, or settle disciplinary matters. Disciplinary matters must be handled as such—disciplinary matters.

Giving Feedback in Real Time

Your organisation probably has several defined mechanisms for giving feedback to employees: coaching sessions, annual reviews, performance interventions, and so on. Each serves an important role. But feedback conversations aren't just a hoop to jump through when these formal appointments roll around. Instead, they should be a continuous practice in your everyday work.

The best time to give feedback, whether positive or corrective, is in the moment. Sharing your real-time reaction to an employee's performance or behaviour allows you to acknowledge what you appreciate and offers the worker a chance to turn her failures into successes right away. It can be stressful to issue corrective feedback, so you may be tempted to hold off until the behaviour occurs again. Don't. Whether you're praising your employees or admonishing them, you will communicate most effectively about the situation when it's fresh in your mind.

Many times, managers become indecisive when things are not moving along the right track, especially when they think the worker is experienced enough to correct the wrongs. They assume that things will be put back in order, only for the managers to be shocked when they notice that the initial error has jeopardised the team's collective success. It is important to be timeous and decisive about corrective feedback and guiding the work when you notice a potential for error that might affect the team's performance. We see this quite often in sports. When your opponent beats your player once or twice, you start guiding that player to course-correct so that error does not cause team defeat.

One of the philosophies I have found to work is to praise in public and criticise in private. By making praise and constructive criticism a routine part of your managerial approach, you create countless new opportunities to track improvements, make adjustments, share resources, and offer support. Here are some scripts to try:

- "This work is excellent. I am impressed. Keep doing great work."
- "There is room for improvement."
- "I am curious to know how you did that."
- "You are genius and are talented. You have great potential."
- "If there is a way I can assist, please feel free to ask."

Giving Difficult Feedback

One of the reasons we avoid giving corrective feedback in the moment is that it can be unpleasant to deliver criticism. Many managers worry that:

- They will be looked at as unpleasant, that this might affect a personal relationship, and/or that the constructive criticism might ignite an emotional reaction, like anger or crying.

- They think the employee will be demotivated further, which will negatively affect the person's self-esteem.
- The problem they need to address touches too closely on the employee's identity and will challenge her sense of self-worth as a competent professional.
- They fear that their feedback might imply the employee's job security is at stake.
- They are uncertain whether they have the courage to give the feedback.

To mitigate these factors, follow these steps:

Step 1: Adopt an objective approach.

Make certain that your interest is in getting great team and organisational results. Also make certain that the main reason you want to give feedback is that you would like to make the necessary corrections timeously. Ensure you have a calm emotional state while offering this kind of feedback so that you do not sound as if you are influenced by anger or negative perceptions. Avoid being personal with the individual. Remove all personal biases. Let your feedback be more developmental and building in nature rather demeaning and destructive. Be open to learning yourself. Ask questions to understand the situation better before offering alternatives. Clarify matters before giving solutions. Ensure that you are not clouded by your or other people's biases. If you are objective, you will be able to notice that the person's difficult personality or diverse experience is causing team conflict, or you will be able to see whether the employees in question have clashing work styles. It might also be that the prevailing culture is dysfunctional and does not accommodate a positive attitude. Focus on performance, behaviour, and attitude ahead of the character of the person. Like the football principle, do not tackle the man; just tackle the ball.

Step 2: Arrange for the conversation.

Prepare for assertive communication that is unemotional. Psychologically clean out any potential sources of negative emotion or insecurity towards the employee. Prepare key points for discussion up front. These could be questions, clarifications, necessary information, behaviour, or the objective of the change to be made. Do not lose sight of the idea that the intention is to build and rectify. This preparation will help you to be smooth during the conversation. Notify the employee ahead of time what will be discussed in the meeting so she can also psychologically prepare herself. Be yourself in the meeting. Do not attempt to be manipulative. Adopt assertive communication all the way. Rehearse ahead of time if you can, by yourself or with a colleague. Role-playing can help you see the situation from your direct report's perspective and figure out what approach will work best. But you must ensure that you maintain originality and authenticity throughout the meeting.

Step 3: Conduct the meeting well.

Any good meeting needs a good introduction that has been preplanned. Try not to waffle in the conversation. Do not mince words. When the meeting begins, do not shy away from jumping into the negative feedback right away. This, though, will depend on how you have introduced the meeting. It is sometimes a good tactic to start the conversation by getting the employee's opinion on the performance. Questions like "Are you happy with your performance right now?" may lead the way. Make the employee feel comfortable in the conversation so the meeting can be fruitful. You may bring up a topic like "I'd like to talk about your production output and the bottlenecks that have been coming up" throughout the meeting to avoid allowing emotions like anger to crop up and influence the outcome of the meeting. Be assertive and candid the whole time, even when you offer corrective feedback.

Step 4: Look ahead.

The feedback must be focused on making future performance better. If there are some behaviours and attitudes that need to be changed, these must be communicated. As with coaching and performance reviews, move the conversation towards an agreement about next steps: "So you'll use the more streamlined approach to the production recordkeeping going forward." If you can't reach an agreement or if the conversation gets too heated, it's OK to press pause: "Let's stop here for now. We can meet again in a week." With a little time, you both might calm down enough to reach an accord. Or the break can give you time to solicit others' input.

Performance Reviews

Most organisations do performance management reviews annually. This is not effective, because an employee will have to wait for twelve months to know how he is performing in his work. In the chapter on performance management, I recommended more regular and frequent performance reviews. I recommend monthly or quarterly performance reviews so that employees do not receive a shock at the end of the year about their performance. Performance reviews must be limited to agreed-upon performance objectives and their associated behaviours—and they must exclude everything else. They must not be used as a trap for disciplinary matters. Disciplinary issues must be handled in separate forums meant for that purpose. As with coaching sessions, you'll use the performance review to discuss goals, provide feedback, and correct performance problems. Unlike coaching, these appraisals directly affect salary decisions, bonus payouts, and promotion decisions. That can make them time-consuming and stressful for the manager and employee alike. Each manager must make sure that they rise above the fear for the benefit of good performance management and also for the good of the company and its success. I have emphasised our preference for 360-degree performance management system as it always results in an objective performance assessment.

If you offer 360-degree performance appraisal feedback, you may want to start by understanding, by asking the employee, why she assessed herself the way she did. You may then share with her how other people have assessed her and then, lastly, how you have assessed her. Then you may want to dwell on areas of disagreement in the assessments and the various comments offered. Maintain a cool frame of mind to offer assertive and constructive feedback. Separate your own personal assessment from the employee's assessment. Avoid saying things like "My boss gave me a rating of 3, so I've given you a 2.5." Confine everything to the agreed-upon performance objectives. Note any new learning from the feedback session. Avoid changing the objectives in the middle of the appraisal period as this might be viewed as a witch-hunt.

The performance review feedback should give your direct report an opportunity for introspection and growth. If it is done frequently enough, it should allow for problems to be addressed head-on. When it comes to the last assessment of the year, there should be no surprises. Everybody should be on the same page with regard to how things have fared that year. Performance review feedback sessions must be done in the most professional way. Your role must be to help the company collect very important information about the individual and the HRM processes of your organisation and to give very important information to the individual. Take minutes during the feedback meetings for potential reference at a later stage. When you give feedback to difficult employees, stay calm the whole time.

Many times, immediately after the superior has completed his appraisal of the employee, he has to immediately give performance review feedback. I have already indicated that I prefer the 360-degree performance assessment system as it ensures objectivity. If only the superior is doing a performance assessment, the chances of that assessment being subjective and inaccurate are very high. I therefore advise all organisations I influence over to adopt this smart way of doing performance reviews. If you have adopted this system, half your challenges have been solved. I also know there are many organisations out there that are still using the old way where one person sits opposite from the other and gives the assessment. In that situation there will be a number of challenges.

Following are steps to take in giving performance review feedback:

Step 1: Prepare your employee.

The employee needs to receive communication that prepares him or her to receive the performance assessment feedback. The appointment must be made well in advance so the employee can prepare for the session as well. The process should have started with reaching an agreement on the performance objectives. The agreement should have been signed at the beginning of the appraisal period. Then the employee will have participated in his or her own self-appraisal. If you are using the 360-degree appraisal system, it is at this point where the employee will receive performance assessment feedback from the other three dimensions, that is from subordinates, peers/customers, and superiors. As I indicated earlier, never cloud your employee's appraisal with your own appraisal. Appraise employees as individuals. Never say, "Because I was given a three by my supervisor, I am going to give you a three also." Though you make your own judgements of your various subordinates, their appraisals must be individualised and objective. That is how you will maintain trustworthiness and respect.

Step 2: Open with a tone of partnership.

Open up the meeting by creating a conducive environment of mutual respect and benefit. Your employee may have an emotional response upon receiving your review, so as your meeting begins, do what you can to put her at ease as you settle in; don't let her feel as if she's in the prisoners' dock about to receive judgement. Assure her that the process is going to be as objective as possible.

Commence with seeking understanding on how the employee has appraised himself. Avoid being subjective and argumentative. When the employee gives you his appraisal feedback, just listen attentively without interrupting. This should help you see things from his point of view and prepare you for the rest of the conversation. Once the employee has finished with his feedback, you may make any clarifications. After that you may share with the employee the collective feedback from subordinates and peers/customers and the overall assessment you conducted. Generally there must be a correlation between your appraisal, subordinates' appraisals, and peers'/customers' appraisals because you all are appraising the employee by the same performance objectives.

Step 3: Open up the appraisal for discussion.

Once you have given all the performance assessment feedback, open up the feedback to discussion. Get the employee to ask questions or make clarifications. Your role will be to summarise the main areas of the appraisal. Give merit where it is due, and highlight areas that require improvement. If there are areas of agreement between the self-appraisal and the overall appraisal, reinforce the employee's perception. If there are areas of disagreement, assert why you have viewed this differently, supporting your view with real evidence based on the actual results. Avoid just focusing on the negative, and by all means try not to make it look like the sandwich technique. Go through each category of appraisal in turn until you arrive at yours.

Once the results of the actual results have been given, then you may direct the conversation to discuss areas of development. Give the employee the opportunity to make recommendations first before you make your own proposals. Identify the gaps, and look for potential remedies to those gaps. Try as much as possible to align with organisational policies, as opposed to using your own personal opinions. For the employees who have really underperformed, create a performance improvement plan for them in line with organisational policy. In most cases such a plan will include the following:

- specific objectives

- a timeline
- action steps
- expected outcome(s)
- required training or resources

Step 4: Sign off and keep records.

After the extensive performance appraisal feedback, you and the employee need to sign off on the amended version of the appraisal, keeping in mind all the agreed-upon contributions to the session. If you need time to amend the contributions, you may schedule a different time for sign-off. If the amendments can be done straightaway, good enough. Sign three copies—one for the employee's record, another for HR, and the other for filing. This final document must include, but is not limited to, the following:

- the name of employee
- the date of appraisal
- key points from your employee's self-appraisal, subordinates' appraisals, and peers'/customers' appraisals
- key points from your appraisal
- a summary of the performance plan
- agreed-on next steps
- performance goals for the coming year

Step 5: Follow up.

The main performance review will be the one done at the end of the year. The other ones will be done to track performance throughout the year. After each performance review, make note of any follow-up that needs to be done with each individual in your team. The high performers will be lined up for opportunities that come their way such as coaching and mentoring, acting in higher positions, doing potential projects, and engaging in talent management activities. The average performers should be engaged in discussions that endeavour to improve their performance. The underperformers should be enrolled in a performance improvement programme (PIP) to improve their performance if the are to stay with the company. Benchmark organisations normally give these people twelve months tops to improve performance, failing which they will be relieved of their duties. These people's performance programme must be monitored closely so that if they need special assistance, it can be rendered timeously.

After your annual performance review discussions, again, make note of any follow-up that is required with each of your team members. For high performers, it might include coaching discussions to prepare them for new responsibilities. Employees who are struggling should be monitored carefully in light of the performance plan you jointly developed. Consider these options for your follow-up:

- monthly follow-up sessions
- training to close up gaps
- guiding the employee on reading material
- coaching and mentoring sessions
- assigning special projects to the employee

The performance review must be treated in the most formal way. You need to document all important matters for record-keeping purposes. Also discipline yourself to be as constructive and objective as possible. The idea is to serve your organisation in the best of the ways and to manage its human resources but also to serve the employees so they may grow in their profession. If you do that, you will make employees respect the process and will also build trust with your team members.

CHAPTER 15

TALENT MANAGEMENT AND SUCCESSION PLANNING

What is talent really? The Oxford Dictionary defines the talent as natural ability or skill. I agree with this definition, but I want to go further and indicate that a skill is a well-developed talent. Talent is a natural ability, but skill is a developed talent. The world is constantly changing, and your organisation is changing along with it. Your team—the company's human capital—drives this change and shapes your company's future. Your role as a manager is to develop talent that meets the needs of your business. This action is fundamentally future-oriented, ensuring you can deliver exceptional performance both today and in the future. Whereas feedback aims to improve performance now, talent development expands your employees' capacities for the future.

I need to acknowledge that talent discovery is not an easy task. People can discover their talents by noticing their passions, interests, energies, abilities, and aspirations. The other important avenue is to listen to other people and their compliments. Sometimes you can be proactive and ask people to give you feedback about the talents and potential they notice in you. Notice the overlaps between positive inner resources and personal capabilities. A friend of mine by the name of Brian Naidoo from Wordworks speaks of the latent ability within the individual. He indicates that an anagram of the word *talent* is *latent*. "Please take a look at the word *latent*," he says. "It is simply *talent*, which is hidden or undiscovered ability."

In any organisation, there can be various kinds of talents—leadership talent, sales and marketing talent, communication and mediation talent, administration and organisation talent, creativity and innovation talent, etc. These kinds of talents and others, when noticed, must be nourished and developed. It is a leader's responsibility to notice and develop talent. I know there are numerous managers who, when they discover unique talents among direct reports, intentionally go all out to destroy those talents because of envy, jealousy, and insecurity. If you notice, these kinds of managers are fired instantly before they destroy the organisation. Great organisations want to keep and nurture their best talents. Great leaders make it their responsibility to do the same for their organisations.

The best managers know how to balance the needs of the organisation with the interests of its employees. As you work with your employees to identify new skills, new experiences, and new areas of interest, you're helping them find work that is fulfilling. As their manager, you must also look for the resonance between their desires and your company's needs. In this chapter, you'll learn about the benefits of employee development and how to spot those opportunities and help your employees take advantage of them.

Employee Development

Benchmark companies that are known for consistently producing sustainable superior profits year after year have one thing in common: they grow and develop the leadership talent of every single person throughout the organisation faster than the competition. They do this by strengthening the capacities of employees at every level to lead in everything they do. Leadership is the one priceless competency that all types of organisations need in modern era. Nonprofit and nongovernmental organisations need to build effective leadership at all levels if they are to achieve their missions. Industrial associations also need to build leaders at all levels. Governments and their various departments also need to build effective leadership at all levels.

It is therefore the absolute responsibility of every manager to develop those reporting to them. It is not a favour but a responsibility. You as the manager must help your subordinates:

- Discover their strengths and passions.
- Discover and improve their talents and skills.
- Advance their aspirations together with their competencies.
- Empower them with challenging tasks and experiences.
- Guide them towards the organisation's pool of coaches and mentors.
- Guide them to deal and cope with change.
- Combine everything they do with the organisation's needs and priorities.

Your work experience and that of your seniors should act as a guideline as to what your direct reports require from you. But it should not be an impediment or limitation to those with high talent. You must also be informed by your organisation's human resources department principles in relation to employee development. Your role is to assist your organisation grow human capital for sustainable success. Your unit also benefits in performance by motivated employees who are growing in their work. Your organisation benefits from having an expanding pool of talented employees and future leaders. The trick is to balance individual and organisational needs. Incompetent leaders will find this difficult because of their insecurity. But competent leaders will never feel insecure about developing their direct reports. They know very well that the more their team members develop, the stronger the team becomes. The stronger the team becomes, the better the results that are produced. Developing your employees also enriches the bonds between them and between them and you. They seem to feel that you care for their success, and hence they feel indebted to contribute to your success.

I often meet with organisations who say that their employees are their greatest asset. In fact, they talk of "human capital", "greatest asset", "talent management", etc. But when I get deeper into the organisation, I notice that these are just PR statements created to deceive board members and other key stakeholders. Talent development and leadership can never take off from the ground if the CEO (or equivalent) and his or her executive team do not have the commitment to make this happen. Remember, leadership is all about observing positive or negative behaviours among those at the top.

My experience with interacting with various organisations is that employee growth is a dominant motivator, larger than monetary incentives. Employees want to feel that their employer cares about their development. And the custodian of this development is the superior above them. In the 1950s, a gentleman by the name of Frederick Herzberg studied employee behaviour at it relates to motivation at work. He came up with what he calls the "two factor" theory. The first one he calls the "hygiene factor", and it includes things like remuneration, organisational policies, interpersonal relationships with leadership, quality of supervision, and working conditions. According to him, the availability of hygiene factors prevents dissatisfaction at work. The second factor is what he calls the "motivator factor", and it includes things like sense of achievement, personal growth, sense of responsibility, challenging and stimulating work, work advancement or progression, and recognition. According to Herzberg, the availability of these factors contributes to employee motivation at work. This analysis then indicates that we must appoint leaders, managers, and supervisors who are capable to providing the motivator factors, assuming that the human resources department will provide the hygiene factors. Many scholars have tried to discredit some aspects of Herzberg's theory, but I fully believe it is still relevant. Those who discredit it do it in defensive of their ineffective leadership.

Development involves acquiring knowledge, skills, and behaviours that improve employees' ability to meet the challenges of a variety of existing jobs or jobs that do not yet exist. Changes in strategy often require changes in the type, level, and mix of skills (Noe et al.).

Employee development is a key contributor to a business strategy based on developing intellectual capital. It helps develop managerial talent and allows employees to take responsibility for their careers. Employee development is a necessary component of a company's efforts to compete in the new economy, to meet the challenges of global competition and societal change, and to incorporate technological advances and changes into the work design. Employee development is key to ensuring that employees have the competencies necessary to serve customers and create new products and customer solutions. Employee development is also important to ensure that companies have the managerial talent needed to successfully execute a growth strategy. Regardless of the business strategy, development is important for retaining talented employees. Also because companies (and employees) must constantly learn and change to meet customer needs and compete in new markets, the emphasis placed on both training and development has increased. Employee commitment and retention are directly related to how employees are treated by their managers. There is a relationship between development, training, and career growth. Look at development approaches, including formal education, assessment, job experiences, and interpersonal relationships. This chapter emphasises the types of skills, knowledge, and behaviours that are strengthened by each development method. Choosing an approach is one part of development planning. Before one or multiple developmental approaches are used, the employee and the company must have an idea of the employee's development needs and the purpose of development. Identifying the needs and purpose of development is part of planning.

Development refers to formal education, job experiences, relationships, and assessment of personality and abilities, all of which help employees prepare for the future. Because it is future-oriented, development involves learning that is not necessarily related to the employee's current job. Traditionally training has focused on helping employee performance in their current jobs. Development prepares them for other positions in the company and increases their ability to move into jobs that may not yet exist. Development also helps employees adapt to changes in their current jobs that may result from new technology, work designs, new customers, or new product markets.

To win the war of talent, managers need to be able to identify high-potential employees, make sure their talents are used, and reassure them of their value before they become dissatisfied and leave the company. Managers also need to be able to listen. Although new employees need direction and bosses who can make quick decisions, they expect to be able to challenge managers' thinking and be treated with respect and dignity. Because of their skills, many employees are in high demand and can easily leave to work for a competitor.

Development activities can help companies reduce turnover in two ways:

1) by showing employees that the company is investing in the employees' skill development and
2) by developing managers who can create a positive work environment that makes employees want to work and contribute to the company goals. One of the major reasons that good employees leave companies is a poor relationship with their managers. Companies need to retain their talented employees or risk losing their competitive advantage. Development activities can help companies with employee retention by developing managers' skills.

There are a number of avenues managers can use to develop their subordinates. These include but are not limited to the following:

- coaching and mentoring
- training
- on-the-job training

- job rotation
- special assignments
- opportunities to act in higher positions

We have already elaborated on training. Let us now explore coaching and mentoring.

Coaching and Mentoring

Coaching is sometimes confused with mentoring. A mentor will generally guide someone based on his own experience, as he has "been there, done that". He will pass on shortcuts and tricks of the trade, and give advice. Successful coaching does not require the coach to have hands-on experience with a client, job, or life situation. In fact, the absence of this experience provides the coach with an objective view of the situation. This is especially important since a coach never gives advice or prescribes a way to reach a certain goal. Coaching is customised for every individual. Let us take a closer look at both coaching and mentoring:

Coaching

Coaching is a one-to-one process and a relationship between an individual and a coach in an effort to enhance or develop the potential in the coachee. The process may be done face-to-face or via telephone. The face-to-face method is effective as the nonverbal aspect of communication is vital to the process. Most formal and professional coaching sessions are carried out by qualified people who work with clients to improve their effectiveness and performance and help them achieve their full potential. Coaches can be hired by coaches or by their organisations. The role of a coach is to facilitate another person's development and performance through a collaborative partnership. A coach does not advise or provide answers to a client's questions. It is a coach's role to focus the client on her best solutions, encourage action, help resolve challenges, provide accountability and momentum, and evaluate outcomes. A coach encourages you to extend yourself and reach your potential through effective goal-setting processes.

Individuals may seek coaching for their personal development, while corporate organisations may offer coaching programmes to their teams to increase the performance of their business. Coaching is a powerful process that provides the momentum to make real, lasting changes. Often at times of transition we ask ourselves "What should I do?" rather than "What do I want?" A coach will ask you effective questions to enable you to focus on your personal priorities and values. He will then assist you in designing a strategy to achieve your aspirations at home and work. Unlike friends and family, coaches are objective and nonjudgemental. They are skilled in listening, effective questioning, and action planning to help you create sustainable changes.

How Does It Work?

The process takes the form of regular meetings between the coachee and the coach. The meetings may be weekly or monthly depending on the agreement between the two parties. Your coach will provide a structure for accountability and support as you work towards your goals and overcome barriers. My most preferred model of coaching is the GROW model. Within the GROW coaching model (create a specific Goal, complete a Reality check, consider Options, and commit to a Way forward), your coach will listen and ask effective questions to help you move forward with the goal.

Each session closes with an agreement to complete certain actions before the next session—homework! Follow-up emails will also be exchanged during this period. The next session will begin with a review of those actions and their results. It is this immediacy and the need to report back that makes coaching so effective.

Working with a coach on a weekly or monthly basis also increases your momentum as you achieve more in a shorter time frame than you would if you were working alone.

You can expect to work with a coach for three months. This is a short enough time to keep focused, but long enough to achieve specific goals. Let us look more closely as the GROW model:

The GROW Model of Coaching

The GROW model gives a simplified, step-by-step methodological approach to the coaching process. It gives the coach a simple guide for following a sequential process that enables achievement. The simplicity of the process gives coaches direction and confidence in handling the coaching responsibility effectively. It ensures perfect organisation for the process and prevents any potential frustrations that the coach may face. Now let us unpack what the GROW model stands for:

G—Goal. The goal represents what it is that needs to be achieved in the simplest and clearest of ways. The goal needs to comply with the business acronym SMART, meaning it needs to be specific, measurable, achievable/attainable, realistic, and time-bound.

R—Reality check. This can otherwise be referred to as "current reality"—where the coachee is right now in relation to the achievement of the goal. If the coachee needs to take several steps to achieve the goal, how many steps has she already taken? This can also be represented as a range from 0 per cent to 100 per cent in the achievement of the goal.

O—Obstacles. Since the coachee really wants to achieve her goal but she has not already achieved it, there must be some obstacles that have prevented her from achieving her goal. What are those obstacles? If these obstacles did not exist, the coachee would have achieved the goal she is after.

or

Options. If the coachee has identified his obstacles, he might also identify or discover possible options he may avail himself of to achieve the goal. What are those options?

W—Way forward. Once the coachee has identified his obstacles and options, he may now be able to craft an action plan to overcome the obstacles. Or he may choose and prioritise the possible options to achieve his goal. This action plan is the way forward to the achievement of the goal.

GROW is simple yet powerful. If y follow the GROW process consistently, it will become a natural process for you. Coaching should be natural. This puts you and your employee at ease, making the process more valuable and rewarding.

Mentoring

Mentoring traditionally involves a more experienced person guiding and passing on her knowledge and experience to others. The mentee could be following in his mentor's footsteps or using her as a role model. Essentially mentoring is about sharing knowledge and experience. The mentoring model has been revised to enable open lines of communication and innovation within organisations through peer and buddy mentoring programmes. Mentorship is a personal developmental relationship in which a more experienced or more knowledgeable person helps to guide a less experienced or less knowledgeable person. The mentor may be older or younger but will have a certain area of expertise. It is a learning and development partnership between someone with vast experience and someone who wants to learn.

The person in receipt of mentorship may be referred to as a protégé (male), a protégée (female), an apprentice, or, in recent years, a mentee.

John Mattone in his book *Talent Leadership* (a must-read) describes the challenges facing human capital/talent management processes in what he terms the four D's: deployment, diagnostics, development, and demarcation.

Deployment Challenges

As I have indicated earlier, there are a lot of instances where recruitment, selection, and production are not based on merit or the competencies required for the job. Sometimes the organisation has situations where there are too many candidates for the position or there are too few candidates for the position. In some situations there is a serious shortage of talent not just within the organisation but also in the labour market. It is important to view selection and promotion as an investment the organisation makes so that you may be able to review the return on investment on your new hire or promotion. A lot of organisations do not do this. In some situations the organisation experiences turnover, but there is not enough talent or fit-for-job for replacement. In others there is a dominant ageing workforce but not a large enough pool of successors. In some organisations, high-potential employees are not identified, or if they are, they are identified inaccurately—or there is favouritism. In some instances there are no succession plans in place. The other deficiency is that the selection and promotion instruments used do not measure the leading indicators such as capability, commitment, and alignment. These instruments are questionable in their validity, reliability, and relevance to the job. The last issue is something Mattone identifies as an inaccurate belief: that the best predictor of future performance is past performance. He says it well this way: "The notion that the best predictor of future behaviour is past behaviour is simply not correct. The absolute best predictor of future behaviour is past behaviour plus overlaying objective assessments plus integrating objective assessments results with perceptions of behaviour plus leveraging the integrated results. All that equals predictable and sustainable performance in leaders, individual contributors and teams."

Diagnostic Challenges

Some organisations find themselves with serious gaps in skills and talent. There is also the issue of a shallow pool of successors at various levels in the organisation. The process of hiring and promoting leaders, managers, teams, and individual contributors is done in a casual manner. There is no return on investment placed on these important hires and/or promotions. People in most organisations are disengaged. I agree with Mattone that the level of engagement is dependent on the quality of immediate supervision coupled with how well the CEO and senior management engage the rest of the organisation. There will obviously be a challenge caused by turnover. The assessment instruments used in most institutions are not aligned with the target competencies required for success, though. The assessment instruments used do not provide accurate diagnostic information relative to strengths and development needs, behaviour feedback, and performance development recommendations. To make matters worse, there is inadequate or no internal (or external) calibration done for the hiring/promotion of leaders and individual contributors. There is limited or no use of multiple diagnostic tools such as the multirater. According to Mattone, a multirater measures communication style assessments, personality assessments, value assessments, simulation assessments, situational judgement assessments, etc.

Development Challenges

In most organisations, information used for the development of employees is always full of discrepancies. An example is when the perceived assessments of actual performance factors are in disagreement with objective assessments of the same performance factors. The other major deficiency is when the training and development is not in any way linked to competencies or assessments. In some situations, there will be long learning or training sessions that take people away from the job for long periods. The development performed in some organisations is not multifaceted and broken into components like coaching, mentoring, training, workshops, on-the-job activities, empowerment, conferences, summits, and e-learning. In some cases individual development planning (IDP) is just lip service. It is either not happening, outdated, not taken seriously, or not based on accurate assessment data. In most cases like this, learners find it difficult to determine how they are progressing in terms of the agreed development goals. In some organisations development is treated as an event as opposed to an ongoing process. Some organisations are so rigid that there is no room for innovation or flexibility. And some have challenges in organisational design.

Demarcation Challenges

The main factor in demarcation is related to performance management and how it is conducted. Many organisations still use top-down performance management as opposed to 360-degree performance management, explained earlier in *Extraordinary Leadership*. Performance management is treated as an event as opposed to being continuous. Many times it is left until the end of the year. Performance management is also regarded as merely a "form" or a piece of "software" to be filled in, as opposed to being treated as a strategic activity in the organisation. Goal setting and performance planning are not aligned to the strategic direction of the organisation. They are also not based on accurate assessments that otherwise might assist in isolating capability, commitment, and alignment. There is no accountability placed on leaders, managers, individual contributors, or teams. In the outputs of performance management, A-team players are not accurately differentiated from the B- and C-team players. The former also receive the same rewards as the latter.

Development Strategies for Your Staff

Effective managers task themselves with the responsibility of helping both employees and their employer mutually achieve their goals. This means establishing the aspirations and interests of subordinates and balancing these out with the opportunities that exist in the organisation. The effective manager must also prevent the organisation from losing the opportunity for advancement in terms of better development of employees. Many companies have their employees undergo psychometric tests for purposes of employee development. Some of these processes, together with performance and recruitment processes, reveal the talents of employees.

Early on in my career, I went through what was termed career path analysis. As part of this, I answered a questionnaire that was meant to establish where I was in terms of or in relation to management development. Most established companies used this kind of strategy to develop their managers. This kind of strategy assisted companies in moving their talented employees or those targeted for promotion through a series of challenging and growth-related positions to prepare them for their potential new assignments. One of the things I appreciated was being moved through divisions that were associated with my next upward movement so I could have experience with each and know what was involved with it. I see this tool as still relevant in modern organisations. But organisations can also adapt flexible organisational structures that allow their upcoming employees to gain multitalented responsibility development.

The career advancement of employees cannot be taken lightly or casually in modern times. Managers must be professionally charged with helping organisations effectively advance the careers of well-performing employees. Those managers who are found hindering this process must be disciplined. Below are a few steps that would guide managers on how to develop their juniors.

Step 1: Have development conversations with your direct reports.

Start with your employees. To support their growth, you need to understand their aspirations and their state of development. The more you know about the people who work for you, the more you will be able to motivate them, coach them, and help them grow. The coaching sessions, performance reviews, and feedback meetings provide many opportunities to gain this understanding.

Step 2: Come up with development interventions.

Once conversations have been had, come up with the possible interventions:

- Get in contact with HR to discuss the development of your direct reports and seek guidance on all available options for each of them. Balance these options with the available budget for investing in employee development. Prioritise all the formal growth opportunities for each individual (including you). This will include training, conferences, seminars, coaching and mentoring programmes, and so forth.
- Investigate all other informal development opportunities such as online courses, webinars, webcasts, live events, books, and audio programmes. Suggest these to your team as additional development material to help them sharpen their skills. Encourage self-funding on some of these. If the organisation can fund them, even better.
- Look for potential projects that can be assigned to various team members as growth opportunities.
- Look for opportunities for temporary secondment, job acting, or job rotation for some of your direct reports targeted at exposing them to new challenges and experiences
- Stretch performance of those direct reports who are meeting current targets with ease. Delegate some of your responsibilities to them for growth purposes.
- Give special assignments to high-potential subordinates, such as innovation champion. Also engage direct reports in benchmarking visits to learn new ways of doing things. For those who get involved in benchmarking visits, give them opportunities to present reports to fellow team members.

The development activities might take people away from work; therefore, this time away must be planned and budgeted for. If temporary replacement or swapping of people is required, let it be done. All participants in these development activities must view and approach them with utmost professionalism for the benefit of all.

Investing in High-Potential Talent

In any team, there will be a small percentage of employees who passionately urge others in terms of performance and willingness to go the extra mile. These employees are classified as high-potential talent. The organisation, through its managers, must assist these high-performing individuals to thrive and to perform even more. Their unique needs must be provided for at all costs. Their talents must be enhanced. These individuals must not be viewed as threats to the managers. They must rather be viewed as special assets to the team, just like any talented sportsperson is viewed in any winning team.

High-potential talented employees are always:

- willing to go the extra mile
- passionate about their work
- striving to consistently produce the best results
- looking for innovation opportunities
- challenging the process for continuous improvement
- viewing constructive feedback positively
- doing what others aren't willing to do
- making the best contributions for the team

High-potential talent are always hungry for knowledge and new learning. They always want to hang around people who uplift them rather those who bring them down or slow them down. They always look for opportunities to become better and perform better. Therefore, they require maximum support and recognition. When they have done something great, they must be recognised and praised. They must feel valued in the team. If these individuals are not appreciated and nurtured, they will go on to greener pastures where they think their careers will grow. So your role as a manager is to be a good steward in helping your organisation to keep such employees. Bear in mind that people do not quit organisations; they quit mediocre managers. So try your best not to be a mediocre manager.

Succession Planning

William Rothwell, author of *Effective Succession Planning*, defines succession planning as "any effort designed to ensure the continued effective performance of an organisation, division, department, or work group by making provision for the development, replacement, and strategic application of key people over time". Succession planning is about identifying talented and/or high-potential employees and developing them in preparation for the potential opening of high-level roles or key positions in the future. It may also be viewed as creating contingency plans for potential loss of key talent in the organisations by proactively developing younger high-potential employees in the present. Organisations that do not have succession plans become reactive when talent losses occur and they are caught unawares. Most organisations have an ageing workforce in key leadership and specialised positions. This ageing workforce has key skills and talents that the younger employees do not have. Succession planning therefore gives the organisation an opportunity to transfer these skills and talents well before the ageing workers decide to retire or move on for other opportunities.

Succession planning and talent management can actually be managed together. They are strategic elements that can only be managed by leaders who have an interest in the long-term success of the organisation. John Mattone's JMP's Succession Management Map serves as an excellent road map to effective succession planning implementation. The critical step is to identify the positions earmarked for succession planning and the people regarded as high-potential talent earmarked for future leadership or the filling of key positions in future. Another important aspect is to classify the people using HR tools such as the 9-box grid or its equivalent together with the latest tools such psychometric tests. Also of paramount importance is the development of individual development plans (IDPs). Performance management assessment and objective and personality assessments are then synchronised into the process for effective implementation.

CHAPTER 16

EFFECTIVELY LEADING TEAMS

Effective teamwork is one of the most important ingredients of broader organisational success. Any team must have a team leader. The leader of the team will be required to manage or lead a number of people to achieve a common or shared goal. One sobering truth is that any existing team is only as effective as its leadership. A team may be involved in a project, serve a function, or have a cross-functional responsibility. The responsibility of the team leadership remains the same in either case. The team leader has the same challenges and opportunities targeted at bringing in unique individual talent for the achievement of ta common goal. The leader therefore has to invest some time in knowing each and every member of his team so as he knows what makes them tick.

The best team is one that works well together. The role of the team leader is to unite different talents, skills, viewpoints, and backgrounds to achieve the common goal. It is important for the leader to understand, value, and positively use the diversity of her team. One important thing the leader must do is to build productive relationships among team members. Another is to get each member to operate at his or her best for the team. A team, therefore, is a group of people striving to achieve a group objective. Leading a team means influencing a group of people to come together.

Having been a sportsperson, I have learnt the importance of team spirit and team culture. If one person works against the team, the team becomes ineffective. One of the most important things is the psychology of team spirit and the oneness of the team. The maximum contribution of each individual in the team is of great importance. Teamwork starts with an initial understanding of what the team's objectives are. Next comes the commitment of each team member to the objectives of the team. One important component of teamwork is communication among the team members. Team members need to communicate about their objectives, their tactics, their challenges, and solutions to their challenges. Another important aspect of teamwork is building competence levels among team members. It is important to determine what skills and competencies are required for the team.

The team leader's job is to ensure that all team members are contributing to their full potential towards the team. Once all team members are contributing to their full potential, the team can be expected to effectively achieve its purpose or goal. It is the purpose of this chapter to guide team leaders on how to build and lead winning teams. A winning team is not necessarily a team composed of the best players. A winning team is a team that is well balanced and has complementary members who are able to collaborate beyond cultural differences and in the face of conflict.

The role of a team leader is to establish an effective team culture and effective team dynamics. An effective team must have the right mix of necessary competencies to achieve its objectives. The work environment in the team must be such that team members communicate freely and are able to perform to the best of their abilities without hindrance or intimidation. Team members must be able to collaborate and support each other, and they must value their diversity as it pertains to the achievement of the team's common purpose. It should not matter whether the leader is starting the team from scratch or whether she inherited an already existing team. These team principles always apply. Some important steps that could be adopted in forming effective teams are as follows:

Step 1: Determine the team purpose.

The team must have a common purpose, goal, or commitment. Without this common purpose, there is nothing binding the team together. A team exists for a purpose. Otherwise you just have a bunch of individuals working randomly alongside each other. Once the team leader has established the team purpose, he can sell it to the rest of the team so they can buy in and believe in it. It is the responsibility of the team leader to ensure each member understands this purpose with the same level of understanding. It must be borne in mind that the purpose of the team may be reviewed regularly to ensure that it is still relevant to the bigger picture of the business.

Step 2: Assemble the team.

First determine the skills and competencies that will be required to achieve the team purpose. If the team is an already existing one, check whether those skills and competencies already exist in the team. If not, or if you are starting a new team, go out and look for those necessary skills and competencies. Ensure there is a good balance of diversity to deal with all potential challenges the team is likely to face. As you build your team, make sure you comply with the principles of good recruitment, selecting, and positioning, which were touched on earlier in *Extraordinary Leadership*. You may have to benchmark, if necessary. Once the team has been built, make sure you fully understand each team member. Know their strengths, weaknesses, preferences, passions, motivations, personal attitudes, skill levels, and life experiences.

Step 3: Set team performance objectives.

Once the team has been assembled, they must then work together to set the team performance objectives in relation to the purpose. The objectives must be set in such a way that they pertain to the team as a unit. Align the team objectives with the overall organisational strategy.

Let the team members understand how their work supports the overall strategy. Determine all the success factors of the team.

Step 4: Establish team ground rules.

The team must work together to set the group norms that will allow for the best team spirit. These norms must be established in a brainstorming session involving the entire team. The ground rules must prevent any discrimination that may come from racial, gender, or ethnic differences. The ground rules should promote diversity of thought or perspective. The rules must also promote effective communication and mutual respect of each member. A win-win mentality must reign in the team.

Step 5: Enhance team bonding and relationships.

Trust is the most important ingredient of a good relationship. Ensure there is trust among all the members. Build a dependence culture in the team. Have regular fun social activities together. Make easy communication channels like WhatsApp groups. Review team performance together. Make each person understand the personality types of the individual members.

CHAPTER 17
FOSTERING INNOVATION

Innovation is no doubt one of the most important business leadership priorities in modern times. Having dealt with many organisations, you notice that most companies have innovation as one of their top priorities in the corporate strategy, but many times this is just lip service and not reflective of the actual reality on the ground. This then brings the question of what the real problem is with having innovation happen on the ground. What I have noticed is that most of these leaders and managers do have a very limited understanding of what innovation really is. I once organised an innovation conference where most of our clients from big organisations had sent their ICT and technology specialists. This gives you a snapshot view of what their understanding of innovation is, namely that is all to do with technology, gadgets, and research and development (R & D). It is indeed true that all these are part of innovation capability, but they are not the only important areas of opportunity for innovation.

But making innovation a priority is not the same thing as making it happen. Many times when management uses the word *innovation*, it is a PR statement leveraged to make the company look smart when in actual fact nothing is happening on the ground. You will see the word used a lot in presentations at company meetings, at board meetings, in corporate advertisement campaigns, and in annual reports. Often there is quite a difference between how you appear to be and how you really are.

In strategy development, the last portion is always an action plan for putting the strategy into real action on the ground. In order to make innovation happen, we need to treat it the same way as implementing a strategy. It is in fact a strategy in its own right. Innovation has helped the most successful organisations around the world to achieve revenue growth by producing a constant stream of breakthrough innovations that compound over time to build a formidable competitive advantage.

For innovation to really happen, it has to be a top strategic priority for the leadership. Top leadership needs to know beforehand what they really want innovation to do for their organisations. Then they have to own the accountability for innovation rather than passing that accountability down to the lower levels. We all know what corporate culture can do to brilliant ideas coming into an organisation. It will eat these brilliant ideas for breakfast. But once innovation has been made part of the corporate culture, then these brilliant ideas can be expected to bring new wealth to the organisation. Many companies around the world have poured money and effort into R & D, expecting it to produce new wealth. But in most instances the responsibility was given to lower employees who had very little influence on the rest of the organisation. This is why most of the time those resources appear wasted as they bring very little to the organisation. For successful business innovation, we must expect business success in the form of sales growth, gross profit, market capitalisation, etc.

In recent history we have seen many companies becoming successful at innovation by changing people's mindsets, dismantling existing industries, or creating new ones—by leveraging a disruptive technology, a radical new product idea, a truly novel service concept, or a game-changing business model. If you look at companies like Apple, you see they have dismantled industries by changing people's mindsets. Many organisations have not been successful at building superior and sustainable end-to-end innovation processes that consistently bring new offerings, establish new markets, win new customers, and drive profitable revenue growth that enables the company to maintain a competitive advantage over the long term.

A trend has been developed by cutting-edge companies around the world that have demonstrated that you do not have to be a technological company to be innovative. We have seen industrial companies winning by tackling innovation challenges and making innovation every employee's business.

Innovation is one of the topics that is close to my heart. I therefore make use of information from my virtual mentors in this area, namely Rowan Gibson and Robert Tucker, renowned authors who write about this topic. Gibson highlights two examples of companies that thrive on innovation and have made it a systemic company-wide strategic tool: GE and P&G. Jeff Immelt took over from Jack Welsh in 2000 and did not want to build company profits through acquisitions and mergers. He chose innovation. He created a timeline of milestones at GE, and the company showed how its innovation strategies adapted to shifting market conditions and technological advances. But the chronology also reveals the unwavering nature of GE's commitment to breaking new ground—taking big steps or small, and eventually adding services as well as products—a stance that has paid off in sustained growth, wealth creation, and global competitive positioning. The consistency of GE's commitment to product innovation was made possible by the steadiness of the company's leadership, say the authors, who point out that the company has had only ten chief executives in its long history. Leader after leader shared a vision for growth that emphasised the "quality, speed, and execution" of GE's innovation efforts. Their involvement went beyond allocating funding; each CEO devoted a great deal of attention to the development of new products, services, and processes in a variety of ways.

P&G is another example that transformed itself by using company-wide innovation. Alan G. Lafley became chairman of P&G in 2000, and he made it clear that he wanted to make innovation everyone's business. He saw innovation as how the company invented, marketed, manufactured, and distributed its products. The reason for this is that, like Immelt, he was under pressure to deliver a relentless level of profit growth each year—and he needed to find imaginative new ways to fuel this growth. He broke down the walls separating product categories, business units, sectors, and brands, thus allowing innovation to flow freely across the entire organisation. More importantly, in 2001 he set a goal for his organisation to source at least 50 per cent of its innovations from outside the company. Thanks to a new organisational model called Connect and Develop, the company had since been able to bring hundreds of new products to the market that had their genesis, in whole or part, outside P&G.

There are a number of companies that have been outright leaders in innovation. Some companies like Apple and Google seem to have been born innovative. But what if your organisation is not one of these innovative companies? What if your firm is a whole lot better at disciplined execution than it is at wealth-generating innovation? If such is the case, then there's only so much you can learn from innovation's "usual suspects". Instead, you need to learn from companies, perhaps like your own, that have transformed from innovation laggards into innovation leaders.

I've done some studies based on the work of people like Rowan Gibson and Robert Tucker that distinguish the real innovation companies. There are certain practices and policies that are meant to make a company a real innovation company. A real innovation company is one that ensures that there is innovation from everyone and everywhere in the company. Some of these practices and policies are:

- Appointment of a high-level executive leader to be primarily in charge of innovation. This leader must also have a dedicated

group of full-time employees responsible for the innovation mandate of the company.
- Creation of a multifunctional or cross-functional innovation team consisting of ten to twelve people from across the company whose mandate it is to generate new ideas and breakthrough proposals around major platforms.
- Appointment of an "innovation board" whose purpose is to screen and fund these proposals with initial funding.
- Ensuring there is company-wide training aimed at developing and distributing the mindset and skills of innovation.
- Ensuring that there is pool of highly trained and visible "innovation champions" in every part of the organisation who are there to guide and mentor any employee who comes up with an idea.
- Ensuring that there is a dedicated IT infrastructure or platform that expedites the spread of new ideas across the company featuring an online idea bank designed to make it easy for employees to share ideas.
- Creation of a comprehensive set of metrics to continually measure innovation performance.
- Ensuring there are annual Innovation Days devoted to recognising and celebrating the work of innovators and featuring awards for the implemented ideas.

By implementing these ideas, a company is aided in coming up with major changes to leader accountability and developing cultural values, resource allocation processes, knowledge management systems, rewards and recognition systems, traditional hierarchy measurements, and reporting systems.

The reason for the large and yawning gap between rhetoric and reality concerning innovation is that most companies have not yet developed a clear model—reflected in management practice—of what innovation actually looks like as a highly distributed, "all the time, everywhere" capability.

The four lenses of innovation, according to Gibson, are these:

- challenging orthodoxies
- harnessing discontinuities
- leveraging competencies and strategic assets
- understanding unarticulated needs

Challenging Orthodoxies

A great way to discover new opportunities for business innovation is by challenging conventional beliefs—or "orthodoxies"—about what drives success in your company and your industry. Orthodoxies tend to become embedded in the way we do business. After a while, they form the dominant logic about the "right" way to compete and to price, organise, market, and develop products and services. Orthodoxies are not by definition "bad" or necessarily *wrong*. In fact, they are often essential to creating a common understanding across a dispersed organisation, allowing teams to work smoothly and efficiently. The problem starts when orthodoxies stifle rather than foster progress—they are potentially limiting if you can't see beyond or around them. If left unchallenged, they may blind you to the possibility of new industry rules, new offerings, and new competitive space. Time and again, the strategy innovations that radically change customer expectations or industry structures come from questioning beliefs that everyone else has taken for granted. To escape from the stranglehold of conventional thinking, you need to systematically question the deeply held dogmas of your company and your industry. Here are four ways to do that:

1) Try to identify and challenge any industry practice that is justified by nothing more than precedent. Think about what would happen if you were to reverse these common industry strategies. Could you imagine alternative ways of doing things? If so, what new opportunities would present themselves? How would customers benefit?

2) Try to spot the absurdities that no one else has spotted, and ask the stupid questions that no one else has asked. Look for things your company does almost habitually every day that are absurd when seen through the eyes of customers. Step back and think about the annoyances, frustrations, and inconveniences that are unwittingly being foisted upon your customers for the sake of the company's own convenience. Then look for solutions.
3) Try looking at any common performance parameter like, say, price, efficiency, or speed of services, and then ask yourself what would happen if you pushed it to a ridiculous limit. Consider how you might dramatically improve that parameter (i.e. not by a factor of $1x$, but by $10x$, or $50x$, or $100x$) by exploring the outer boundaries of what is possible. If you were to do that, how would customers benefit?
4) Look for situations where the customer is getting a benefit on the one hand but simultaneously losing out somewhere else, and try to take the negative out of the equation. Ask yourself how you could turn a win-lose situation into a win-win.

Innovation leaders must always challenge the process. They must seek and accept the challenge. The challenge might be an innovative new product, a cutting-edge service, a groundbreaking piece of legislation, an invigorating campaign to get adolescents to join an environmental programme, a revolutionary turnaround of a bureaucratic military programme, or the start-up of a new plant or business. All cases involve a change in the status quo. Not one person claims to have achieved a personal best by keeping things the same. All leaders challenge the process.

Leaders are pioneers, people who are willing to step out into the unknown. They search for opportunities to innovate, grow, and improve. Leaders are not always creators or originators. Innovation comes from listening more than it does from telling. Product and service innovations tend to come from customers, clients, vendors, people in the labs, and people on the front lines. Process innovations come from people doing the work.

The leader's primary contribution is in the recognition of good ideas, the support of those ideas, and the willingness to challenge the system to get new products, processes, services, and systems adopted. Leaders also pay attention to the capacity of their constituents to take control of challenging situations and become fully committed to change. You can't exhort people to take risks if they don't also feel safe. Leaders learn by leading, and they learn best by leading in the face of obstacles.

Harnessing Discontinuities

According to Gibson, radical innovators are always looking for discontinuities in the way business is done. These innovators look for various unrelated patterns of developing trends in the external environment and search for opportunities that might change competition or restructure industries. There may be a convergence of developing bundles of change in society such as demographics, lifestyles, consumer needs, legislature, or technology. These are potential openings for future bundles of change in the business landscape. There may be areas that competitors are not looking at or are ignoring. There may be areas where they are underestimating. The innovators in this space will look for the momentum and how these changes could be influenced and amplified to shape the future. They take advantage of patterns of change or intersections of changes. They look for areas of imminent change that can be filled with new innovations. People leverage on discontinuities by exploring where their competitors are not exploring, by looking for even weak signals and then amplifying them for major consequences, by understanding historical trends and seeing how they impact the present, and by exploring change intersections.

Leveraging Competencies and Strategic Assets

A third method for generating insights that lead to radical innovation is in trying to leverage your company's embedded resources—its core competencies and strategic assets—in completely new ways. Instead of viewing your company in terms of business units and organisation charts, try to reimagine it as a portfolio of competencies and strategic assets.

Let me make the distinction clear. By "core competencies", I mean things that your company *knows* how to do uniquely well—its skills and unique capabilities. By "strategic assets", I mean things that your company *owns*—brands, patents, infrastructure, customer database, proprietary standards, and anything else that is both rare and valuable.

Unfortunately, most companies define themselves by what they do, rather than by what they *know* or what they *own*. Usually they find it difficult to see things like skills, processes, technologies, assets, and values as distinct, stand-alone entities because they are completely embedded in the company's current business model. But radical innovators have the ability to decouple particular skills and assets from the existing business and then leverage them in new ways or in new settings to generate growth opportunities.

The fact is, radical innovators tend to think of the whole world as a Lego kit of different competencies and strategic assets, owned by different companies, which can potentially be reconnected like building blocks or used in a new context to invent novel products, processes, services, and business models. These innovators then use their company's unique competencies and assets as big opportunities for innovation to produce new products, services, or business models.

They identify unique *core competencies* by identifying the strengths that meet the following criteria:

- creating value for the customer
- being unique or at least scarce
- being sustainable over a significant period of time
- being important to the company's position today
- having the ability to be leveraged into new products, markets, or businesses

They then identify *strategic assets* by doing the following:

- determine which of their company's assets are rare, are valuable to customers, and can be used to create new opportunities
- exploit strategy assets in new ways to bring value to customers
- explore whether their strategic assets can be valuable in other industry settings
- imagine alternative uses of their strategic assets in building new business models

Understanding Unarticulated Needs

The fourth way to discover new insights for radical innovation is to address unsolved customer problems, unvoiced needs, and market inefficiencies. The ability to spot an unmet customer need—not only before the competition but also before the customer is even aware of it or articulates it—can lead to significant innovation opportunities.

Radical innovators are deeply empathetic; they understand—and feel—the unvoiced needs of customers. They recognise needs that customers don't even know they have yet, or they solve some common frustration in a way that people could never have imagined, which is precisely why they are not articulating the need or asking for a specific product, service, or business to address it.

You will rarely uncover deep, unarticulated customer needs and frustrations by conducting traditional market research—that is asking customers to answer a questionnaire, either on paper, online, or by phone. It's also unlikely you will discover these needs or frustrations by going out and directly asking customers what they want. Usually, customers will give you obvious answers like "I want it cheap" or "It should be easy to buy and use" because they are generally only thinking in terms of the solutions and choices that are already available on the market. Most customers are prisoners of their experiences and of their understanding of how a particular service or product is usually delivered.

If you truly want to understand customers' wants and needs, you need to remove the distance between you and them. You need to "get into the customer's skin" by immersing yourself in their environment and by making their needs, frustrations, and desires your own. Try to develop an empathetic understanding of the customer's situation. Somehow, you want to "become" the customer, to feel the customer's experience, to identify and understand the customer's problems, and then look for ways to solve them.

Here are three effective methods you can use:

1. Spend time with your customers. Try to understand that many breakthrough innovation opportunities are found not by looking at the product but by looking at the customers and users. Use the power of direct observation—which means getting out of the office and into the field, "shadowing" the customer from multiple vantage points, and making photo or video diaries.
2. Map the entire customer experience—from the first contact with your company right through to the final bill you send. At several stages of the demand chain, you will usually find that the customer has significant needs, problems, and frustrations. Ask yourself: "What if we made the customer's problem our problem?"
3. Look for analogies from other industries. Are there customer needs that other industries/products/businesses fulfil that your company has not yet been responsive to? How are these other industries and markets solving customer problems and reshaping customer expectations? Could you use these analogies to create a more ideal customer experience in your own industry?

Robert Tucker is another authority on innovation I have been following. I actually invited him to present at my event in 2013. He has done a lot of research into innovation. In his research, some companies come out as more superior on innovation than others. He terms these the "innovation vanguard". The comparison between the innovation vanguard and other companies is that the vanguards seek out the unmet and unarticulated needs of their customers and teach themselves how to listen differently from everyone else. They master the art of scanning for insights into their customers and anticipating their needs and wants often before the customers themselves know what is it they will respond to. Tucker emphasises that for innovation to be a success, it needs to be treated as a disciplined process. There needs to be a systematic way of collecting ideas. It must be a priority for the senior management team to harvest and nurture ideas on an ongoing basis. The company must involve all its influential people, including top management, in the innovation process. A culture of experimentation must be entertained. Management must provide funds and other resources for people to work on the ideas.

Innovation must not be only the responsibility of one small department. It must be approached comprehensively throughout the company. Innovation must be made part of the DNA of the organisation. It must include an organised, systematic, and continual search for new ideas and opportunities. All the innovation efforts must be centred on the customer. They must think of the customer in everything they do, in an effort to impress the customer. In other words they must live and breathe the customer. Vanguard companies create and enforce a culture of innovation. The leadership learn, and allow all their employees to learn, the seven fundamental skills of innovation, which are as follows:

1. **Embrace the opportunity.** Each individual must embrace the opportunity mindset in every task they work on and every project they are part of.
2. **Become an assumption assaulter.** Each individual must be adept at assaulting assumptions: personal, organisational, and industry-wide.

3. **Cultivate a passion for the end customer.** Each individual must have a passion for the end customer, whether internal or external.
4. **Think ahead of the curve.** Each individual must be able to think ahead of the curve with regard to emerging trends, threats, and opportunities.
5. **Become an idea factory.** Each individual must know how to fortify the idea factory and discover the ideas needed to propel their team/workgroup and organisation forward.
6. **Become a standout collaborator.** Each individual must be considered a standout collaborator by their peers and organisation by virtue of the value they add on a consistent basis.
7. **Build the buy-in for new ideas.** Each individual must be adept at building the buy-in for their ideas and enrolling others in their vision.

Let us now look into the kind of leadership responsibilities that will ensure that innovation is a success in an organisation. As indicated earlier, the key is to design and implement an organised process for innovation. The new approach to innovation must be directed from the top and engage the entire organisation. It must be focused on adding new and unique value to the customer through the introduction of new products, services, and business models. Robert Tucker also indicates that leadership must adopt a number of strategies if innovation is to be successful. These strategies are as follows:

Leadership Strategy 1

Innovation must be led from the top. It must also be supported by the top of the organisation, if you are to get the buy-in you need. Because of its complexity, innovation needs to be the top priority of senior management in your company while a new approach is conceived and implemented. The top team must take the lead and establish innovation goals. The top team must figure out how to involve people in contributing ideas and break down the silos that prevent collaboration and experimentation. And the team is the unit that needs to establish milestones and metrics to gauge progress along the way.

Leadership Strategy 2

Design and implement an innovation process. The first thing that needs to be done in as far as implementing the process goes is to define innovation in language that everyone in the organisation is able to understand. The definition must be clear to everyone. All the behaviours that leadership would like to encourage must be clearly spelled out. All the growth goals that the organisation would like to attain must also be clearly spelled out. A process for channelling people's ideas must be provided. There must a plan to overcome any barriers that may crop up and hinder innovation in the organisation. Innovation must be fully embedded in the organisation. There must be someone appointed as the innovation leader, and this person must report to the CEO or equivalent.

Leadership Strategy 3

Spread out responsibilities for making innovation happen. All the innovation expectations must be clearly spelled out. All the required innovation behaviours must be publicised. A curriculum for innovation must be created. The organisation must provide basic training for creativity. Advanced training on innovation must be provided to select groups that are closely working on innovation or to the innovation champions.

Leadership Strategy 4

Allocate resources and decide on levels of risk. The leadership must budget for and provide resources for innovation to happen. There must be financial resources for experimentation on an idea. Top leadership must make decisions on the level of risk to be tolerated in the innovation implementation.

Leadership Strategy 5

Establish innovation metrics. The top leadership must establish the metrics that will be used to measure innovation success. One of the most important of these metrics is to measure the percentage of revenue received from new products and services. There can also be metrics to measure the pipeline, that is the number of good ideas not yet implemented. This will demonstrate how effective the people are at coming up with ideas. While measuring metrics, the leadership must avoid creating disunity among the employees.

Leadership Strategy 6

Reward and incentivise innovation. For innovation to be a success, the right behaviours must be rewarded and incentivised. This demonstrates seriousness of the implementation process. The rewards can be in the form of financial incentives or just in the form of recognition. Financial incentives can be either intrinsic or extrinsic. But intrinsic incentives carry more power in that they prove commitment. One might take recognition lightly, but if a top leader shows interest in the new idea brought forward, it carries with it a huge amount of encouragement. Ordinary employees want to be seen as adding value. If you show interest and appreciation, this can give the motivation for individuals to continue to bring forth good ideas.

CHAPTER 18

LEAVE A GREAT LEGACY

Real extraordinary leadership requires work on your spiritual life, polishing that connection to the highest part of you so that you dedicate your best years at work to doing deeds that will last beyond your death. Most people don't discover how to live until just before they die. During their best years, too many people live in a walking coma. They are not really conscious of what's truly important in life: showing leadership, actualising your potential, and doing your part to change the world through the work you are doing and the person you are becoming. When they are confronted with a wake-up call of their imminent end, these sleepwalkers start to dig beyond the superficial and go deep. They begin to realise that at birth they'd received stunning talents and precious gifts, along with a corresponding responsibility to polish that genius so that they could express it over the course of their lives and elevate the lives of everyone around them in the process. In this materialistic world, we chase titles, fast cars, and big bank accounts in search for greatness, when in truth all that we really want, we already have. The excellence and happiness we crave is inside us. We are looking for it all in the wrong places, in position, in social status, and in things like net worth. But before we know it, each of us will be dust. And the street sweeper will be buried next to the CEO. There is no difference in their graves: same size hole and no first-class site or different route to get in.

Leaders who leave a great legacy are leaders who make a tremendous positive difference. One of the keys to arriving at the end of your life without regrets is doing the work of creating a lasting legacy. These types of leaders intend to create a better world within their sphere of influence. How? First they recognise that what they do daily, over time, becomes their legacy. Second, they decide early in their lives what kind of legacy they want to leave. They decide how they want to be remembered. They decide what they would like people to say about them at their funeral. It is never too late to leave a great legacy. If you think your life has been mediocre up to this point, it is fine to recognise that. You can now set off in the right direction and begin to change the way you live, starting today. You can start to determine your purpose, meaning, and significance in life. You can craft a vision along those lines and start acting on it before it is too late. Legacy can be generally debated and discussed. But the truths are always in the open even though some people try to ignore them. You can test this idea on any leader who you thought has left a great legacy.

The people who have a great legacy are people who live their lives with a defined purpose. They are not people who take their lives casually. They know that they are here on this earth for a reason. They identify that reason and attempt to live it with all their effort and will. These people regard life as a blessing from God. They are thankful for that blessing and treat it with respect.

In my book *Become Extraordinary*, I have emphasise coming upon or discovering one's life's purpose. My reason for this is that life is not meant to be taken casually, because it was given for a reason by the Creator. I have indicated that there are two important days in your life—the day you were born and the day you discover why you were born. When you discover your purpose for life and you live it, you come to a point where you leave a great legacy with your life. A powerful purpose always helps a person to write a powerful eulogy ahead of time. Living that purpose makes the purpose of life become to leave a great legacy. All people who left a great legacy behind identified with a powerful purpose and committed themselves to it.

Somebody who leaves a legacy is somebody who has tried to become a servant of the people in a selfless way. From the leadership perspective, it is someone who has provided servant leadership with absolute moral authority. The people we think of who fit this mould are the likes of Nelson Mandela, Mother Teresa, Abraham Lincoln, and Albert Einstein.

Somebody who leaves a legacy is someone who has come out of the ordinary in an extremely positive way. People appreciate what the individual has done for them for the rest of their lives. These people also become heroes of history for the great things they have done.

When I was writing this chapter, I had the opportunity to listen to the celebration of the centenary of Nelson Mandela. The theme of the occasion was Renewing the Mandela Legacy and Promoting Active Citizenship in a Changing World. There were speeches that I felt were relevant to this edition. These are snippets of what was said about him by various speakers:

- Mandela would suppress his inner fears in order to be brave for other people so as to create peace.
- His incredible uniqueness was that he was a humble and honest man—a symbol of selflessness, a humble servant of the people. He had character and integrity.
- He would take risks, make sacrifices, and provide service—seeing the world as it should be seen. He was a man who earned the respect of all, a global icon who demonstrated what it means to be human. He had appeal beyond lines of colour, class, race, and gender.
- He is one of history's true giants. He had a strong sense of self-determination. He fought for freedom, justice, and equal

opportunity. He promoted hope for a better life and greater possibilities.
- His power grew while the power of his jailers diminished. One thing he believed is that people learn to hate. But people can be taught to have love because love comes naturally to the human heart.
- Basic truths do not change. Democracy means the government exists to serve the people and not the other way around. Democracy also means engaging people who hold different views from you. To make peace with the enemy, one has to work with the enemy so that the enemy becomes a partner.

Just consider the conclusion of a three-hour speech given by Nelson Mandela on 20 April 1964 from the dock at the Rivonia Trial. The speech is considered one of the greatest speeches of the twentieth century and a key moment in the history of South African democracy. That conclusion is as follows: "During my lifetime I have dedicated my life to this struggle of the African people. I have fought against white domination, and I have fought against black domination. I have cherished the ideal of a democratic and free society in which all persons will live together in harmony and with equal opportunities. It is an ideal for which I hope to live for and to see realised. But, My Lord, if it needs be, it is an ideal for which I am prepared to die."

Leaders who leave a great legacy live for something bigger than themselves. They have great personal and family lives, but they impact a wide variety of people. They are significant to a variety of lives. They make their lives matter and are of use to as many people as possible. In my emotional intelligence training sessions, I spend the last day helping my delegates to draft their personal mission statements. I urge them to dig deep in their subconscious mind and discover the legacy they would like to leave to their coworkers, customers, family members, friends, and community. The essence of the exercise is to design the kind of tribute you would like each of these groups of people to give you at your funeral. The outcome is always amazing. Robin Sharma says, "This is how each of us can shift from the realm of the ordinary into the heights of the extraordinary. And walk among the best who have ever lived." Let us also take a look at this powerful Sanskrit saying: "When you were born, you cried while the world rejoiced. Live your life in such a way that when you die, the world cries while you rejoice."

We have looked at how some presidents like Nelson Mandela can leave a great legacy. Let us also look at how an ordinary person can make a great difference in her community and leave a great legacy. To close this chapter, I want highlight a certain extraordinary human being I learnt about from one of Robin Sharma's presentations. This woman's name is Oseola McCarty. She was born on 7 March 1908 and died on 26 September 1999. She had to drop out of school at grade six to take care of her aunt who was sick and needed care but did not have children of her own. She spent all her life as a cleaner (like her grandmother) in Hattiesburg, Mississippi, until 1994, when she was forced to retire because of arthritis. She was never married and had no children of her own. She supported her grandmother who died in 1944, her mother, who died in 1964, and her aunt who died in 1967. At an early age, though uneducated, she was taught to save money by her mother. She opened several savings accounts at various area banks. At some point, she appointed the Trust National Bank as a trustee for her savings accounts and her estate. She lived a simple life. She had no car, she walked everywhere she went, she pushed a shopping trolley a mile when she bought her groceries, she rode with friends to church, she never bought newspapers, and she owned a black-and-white television, just to mention a few things. The house she lived in was given to her by her uncle. She received money from her aunt and mother when they died, and she channelled the money into her savings accounts. Over the years her savings accumulated, and her trustee (the Trust National Bank) gave her consistent advice. With the assistance of a local attorney she cleaned for, she planned her estate in this way: 10 per cent to her church, 10 per cent to each of her three remaining relatives, and the remaining 60 per cent to be used for African American students who could not receive an education because of financial challenges, through the University of Southern Mississippi.

The news about her plan broke in July 1995 and attracted global attention. Her overall savings at the time were US$150,000, accumulated from her meagre earnings. Harvard University and Southern Mississippi University awarded her with honorary degrees in 1996 and 1998 respectively. She was also presented with a Presidential Citizens Award by President Bill Clinton and with scores of awards and honours from other authorities. She also received the United Nations' Avicenna Medal for her contribution to the education of the underprivileged. She died of cancer in September 1999.

What a soul! This is just one example of a person who left a lasting positive legacy. In our small way, and depending on the gifts we have been blessed with, we can live extraordinary lives and demonstrate extraordinary leadership. Good luck!

REFERENCES

Covey, Stephen R., *The 8th Habit* (New York: Free Press, 2004).

Collins, Jim, Good to Great (London: Random House Business Books, 2001).

Goleman, Daniel, Emotional Intelligence (London: Bloomsbury Publishing Plc, 1996)

Harvard Business Review, *Harvard Business Review Manager's Handbook: The 17 Skills Leaders Need to Stand Out* (Boston: Harvard Business School Publishing Corporation, 2017).

Kassa, Biniam. *The Impact of Human Resource Management Practice on Organizational Performance: A Study on Debre Brehan University, Ethiopia* (2016).

Kouzes, James M., and Barry Z. Posner, *Leadership Challenge* (3rd edn, San Francisco: Jossey-Bass, 2002).

Mattone, John, *Intelligent Leadership: What You Need to Know to Unlock Your Full Potential* (New York: AMACOM, 2013).

———— *Talent Leadership: A Proven Method for Identifying and Developing High-Potential Employees* (New York: AMACOM, 2013).

Maxwell, John C., *The 5 Levels of Leadership* (New York: Hachette Book Group, 2011).

Nel, P. S., P. S. van Dyk, G. D. Haasbroek, H. B. Schultz, T. Sono, and A. Werner, *Human Resources Management* (6th edn, Cape Town, 2003).

Noe, R. A., J. R. Hollenbeck, B. Gerhart, and P. M. Wright, *Human Resources Management* (5th edn, New York, 2006).

Robbins, Anthony, Awaken the Giant Within (London: Simon & Schuster, 1992)

Rothwell, William, Effective Succession Planning: Ensuring Leadership Continuity and Building Talent from Within (4th Edition, New York: AMACOM, 2010)

Sharma, Robin, The Leader Who Had No Title (London: Simon & Schuster, 2010)

Skaarzynski, P., and R. Gibson, *Innovation to the Core: A Blueprint for Transforming the Way Your Company Innovates* (Harvard Business School Publishing, 2008).

Thompson Jr., A. A., A. J. Strickland III, and J. E. Gamble, *Crafting and Executing Strategy* (15th edn, New York: McGraw-Hill/Irwin, 2007).

ABOUT THE AUTHOR

Joseph K. Pheto is the founding director of Jorisma, a company registered in Botswana, that offers training, business conferences, motivational speaking, personal and professional coaching, team building, and business consultancy to a range of clients around his native country. He is also the author of the book *Become Extraordinary*.

He organises and speaks at conferences and presents at seminars and workshops. He has hosted renowned international speakers and authors such as Dr John C. Maxwell, Robin Sharma, Dr John Demartini, Robert Tucker, John Mattone, and Dr David Molapo.

Joseph graduated with honours as an engineer from University of Exeter in England and worked for fifteen years in Botswana's mining industry. He rose up the ranks from a graduate trainee to a divisional manager until he decided to change careers to become a people developer. Joseph is accredited by the Botswana Qualification Authority as a full-time trainer on a number of topics, including leadership, emotional intelligence, coaching, change management, sales and marketing, entrepreneurship, and managing small businesses. Joseph's services have been sought for various organisational endeavours such as strategic reviews, strategy development, strategy implementation, motivation, training, team building, and coaching. He is a certified coach by the International Labour Organisation's International Training Centre (ICT). He is also a certified neurolinguistic programming (NLP) practitioner and a coach with credentials from the NLP Institute in New York. He conducts personal and professional training in his home country of Botswana.

Joseph K. Pheto

Joseph is a former executive vice president of Junior Chamber International (JCI). He was also honoured with JCI senatorship in 2005 for his outstanding contribution to this international nongovernmental organisation committed to creating positive change in global societies by providing development opportunities that empower young people to create such change. He also has a heart for community development. He is a president of a soccer club in his own village and has served his church, the Catholic Church, in various ways, including as a parish chairman.

If you want to make bookings for training, speaking, or any of the services the author offers, you may make contact with the Jorisma Events Company:

Telephone: (267) 393-0521

Fax: (267) 393-0519

Cell: (267) 721-42491

Email: info@jorisma.co.bw

Website: www.jorisma.co.bw

www.ingramcontent.com/pod-product-compliance
Lightning Source LLC
Chambersburg PA
CBHW030936180526
45163CB00002B/592